ROBERT B. GARDNER, Publisher
Bob Colgate, Editor
NFHS Publications

To maintain the sound traditions of this sport, encourage sportsmanship and minimize the inherent risk of injury, the National Federation of State High School Associations (NFHS) writes playing rules for varsity competition among student-athletes of high school age. High school coaches, game officials and administrators who have knowledge and experience regarding this particular sport and age group volunteer their time to serve on the rules committee. Member associations of the NFHS independently make decisions regarding compliance with or modification of the playing rules for the student-athletes in their respective states.

NFHS rules are used by education-based and non-education-based organizations serving children of varying skill levels who are of high school age and younger. In order to make NFHS rules skill-level and age-level appropriate, the rules may be modified by any organization that chooses to use them. Except as may be specifically noted in the NFHS Football Rules Book, the NFHS makes no recommendation about the nature or extent of the modifications that may be appropriate for children who are younger or less skilled than high school varsity athletes.

Every individual using the NFHS football rules is responsible for prudent judgment with respect to each contest, athlete and facility, and each athlete is responsible for exercising caution and good sportsmanship. The NFHS football rules should be interpreted and applied so as to make reasonable accommodations for athletes, coaches and officials with disabilities.

2013 High School Football Rules Simplified & Illustrated

Produced by Referee Enterprises Inc., publishers of Referee magazine.

Published by the
NATIONAL FEDERATION
OF STATE HIGH SCHOOL ASSOCIATIONS
PO Box 690
Indianapolis, IN 46206
Phone: 317-972-6900, Fax: 317.822.5700
www.nfhs.org

ISBN-13: 978-1-58208-214-1

Printed in the United States of America

Table of Contents

       Each state high school association adopting the NFHS football rules is the sole and exclusive source of binding rules interpretations for contests involving its member schools. Any person having questions about the interpretation of NFHS football rules should contact the rules interpreter designated by his or her state high school association.

       The NFHS is the sole and exclusive source of model interpretations of NFHS football rules. State rules interpreters may contact the NFHS for model football rules interpretations. No other model football rules interpretations should be considered.

2013 NFHS Football Rules Changes

Rule Changed	Rule Change Description
1-5-3a(5)a	Solid-colored towels now legal.
1-6	Use of communication devices expanded.
2-4-1	Definition of a catch clarified.
3-5-10d	Loss of helmet after the down clarified.
6-5-6 PENALTY; 2-9-2; 5-2-1, 2; 6-5-4; 10-4-2b	Kick-catching interference penalty added.
7-5-10 PENALTY; Table 7-5	Pass interference penalties revised.
8-3-3	Score on a try clarified.
9-3-8c (NEW)	Blocking on free kicks revised.
9-4-3l (NEW)	Initiating contact with a helmet-less opponent is now an illegal personal contact foul.
9-6-4g (NEW)	Players continuing to play without a helmet is now illegal participation.

2013 Editorial Changes

Field Diagrams; 1-2-3b NOTES 2; 1-2-3f; 1-2-3l; 1-5-2b; 1-5-3c(2); 1-5, 1-6 PENALTY (Deleted); 1-7; 2-6-2a, b; 2-13-2; 2-32-5b; 2-34-2; 3-5-8c; 3-6-3; 6-5-4; 7-5-2c; Table 7-5-2e; 9-3-8; 9-3 PENALTY; 9-4 PENALTY; 9-6 PENALTY; 9-8-1f NOTE; 9-8-1g, h; 9-8 PENALTY; 10-4-2b; 10-6; Football Fundamentals – II-4, 5, IX-6, X-3e, 6-8; Resolving Tied Games – 10-4-3; 3.1.1 Situations G, H, I; Nine-, Eight- and Six-Player Rules Differences; PENALTY SUMMARY; Official Football Signals – 40, 43.

Points of Emphasis

(For complete discussion of the 2013 points of emphasis, see page 27)

1. Prohibition On Contact to and With the Helmet
2. Reconditioning and Recertification of Football Equipment
3. Free Blocking Zone Enforcement — Consistent Enforcement of Blocking Below the Waist

Part 1

2013 New or Revised NFHS Rules

This simplified and illustrated book is a supplement to the 2013 NFHS Football Rules Book. As such, it is intended to aid in the administration of the game and in the standardization of interpretations through a unique method of presenting rules.

Each year the NFHS Football Rules Committee considers many items which are submitted as potential changes or revisions. The items which were approved by the NFHS Board of Directors are listed on pages 6 and 7. The majority of illustrations in Part 1 show those changes and revisions.

The NFHS Football Rules Committee also identified areas of concern which are designated as "Point of Emphasis" for the current season. It appears in Part 2.

The illustrations found in Part 3 of this book have been revised to reflect any changes or clarifications as directed by the NFHS Football Rules Committee. Recent interpretations have been added to keep the contents current.

1-5-2b Gloves must meet the NOCSAE test standard at the time of manufacture with visible stamp as above, unless made of unaltered plain cloth.

1-5-3a(5)a Towels shall be one solid color but not ball- or penalty flag-colored and may have no more than one visible manufacturer's logo/trademark reference that does not exceed 2¼ square inches in any dimension. Not every player has to wear a towel (PlayPic A). But if any player wears a towel, teammates must wear the same, solid color towel. The towels in PlayPic B are illegal.

1-6 Communication devices may be used by coaches and nonplayers on the sidelines as long as they are not used to communicate with players (PlayPic A). It is illegal to use those devices to communicate with players inside the 9-yard marks, as in PlayPic B.

1-6 During an outside the 9-yard marks conference (PlayPic A), the coach may show players an electronic device. During an inside the 9-yard marks conference, a coach may use the device (PlayPic B) but not show it to players (PlayPic C).

2-4-1 In PlayPic A, the airborne receiver is contacted so that his forward progress is stopped. When the defender carries him out of bounds (PlayPic B), the result is a completed pass.

2-4-1 When an airborne receiver is contacted by a defender (PlayPic A), causing him to make first contact with the ground out of bounds (PlayPic B), it is an incomplete pass. The game official's judgment regarding whether A1 would have landed inbounds is not a factor.

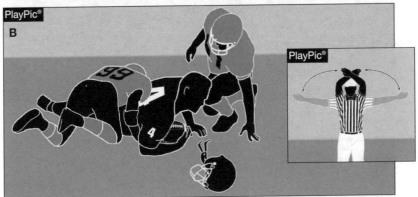

3-5-10d The runner is contacted by opponents (PlayPic A). When the runner comes to the ground, his helmet comes completely off his head and an official's time-out ocurs (PlayPic B). Because the helmet came off during continuing action, the player must sit out for one down (PlayPic C).

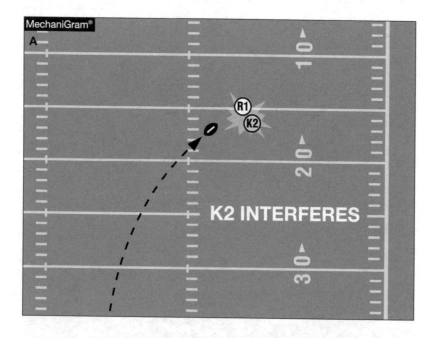

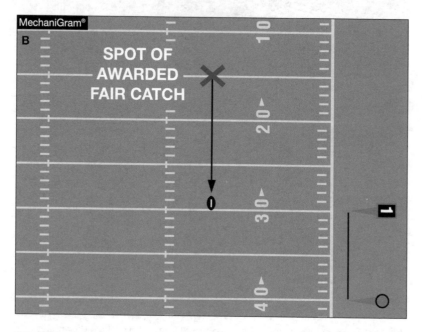

6-5-6 Penalty K commits kick-catching interference (MechaniGram A). If R chooses an awarded fair catch, the 15-yard penalty may be enforced from the spot of the awarded fair catch (MechaniGram B).

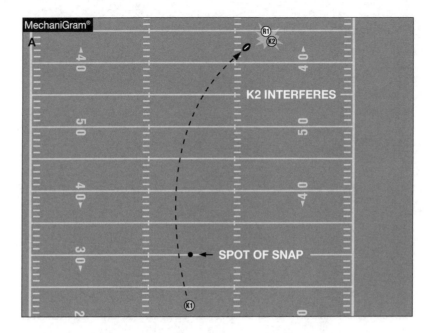

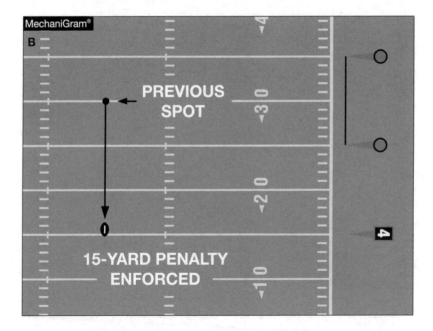

6-5-6 Penalty K commits kick-catching interference (MechaniGram A). R may choose enforcement of the 15-yard penalty from the previous spot and a replay of the down (MechaniGram B).

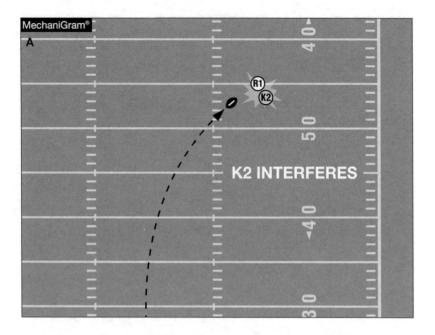

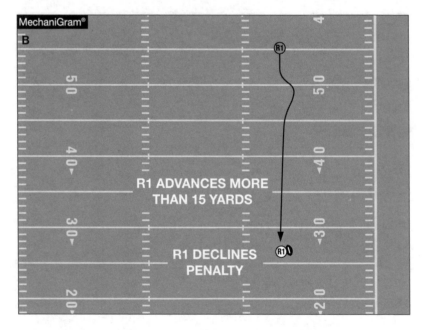

6-5-6 Penalty K commits kick-catching interference (MechaniGram A). R may choose to decline the penalty and take the result of the play (MechaniGram B).

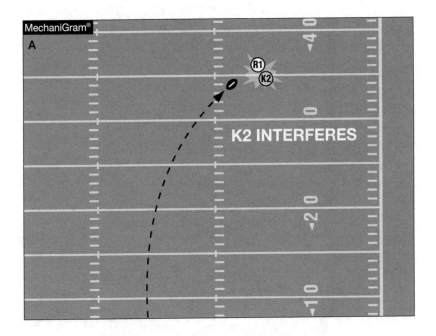

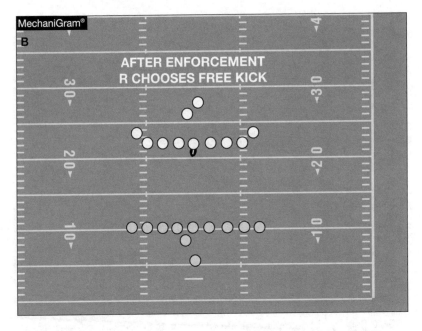

6-5-6 Penalty K commits kick-catching interference (MechaniGram A). If R chooses an awarded fair catch, the 15-yard penalty may be enforced from the spot of the awarded fair catch. R may then choose a free kick (MechaniGram B).

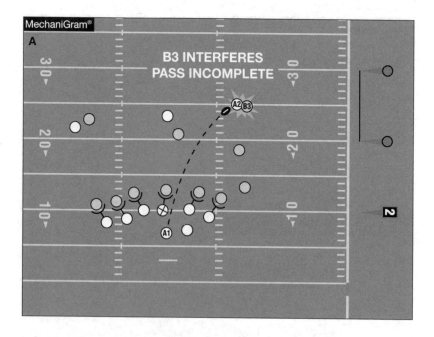

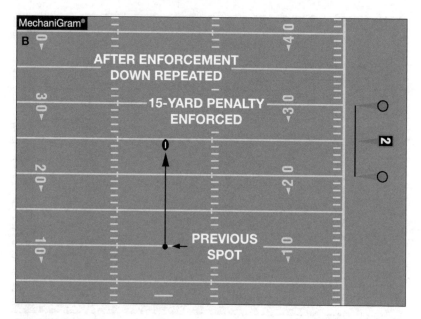

7-5-10 Penalty The automatic first down portion of the penalty for defensive pass interference has been removed. When B commits pass interference (MechaniGram A), the down is replayed after enforcement of a 15-yard penalty from the previous spot (MechaniGram B).

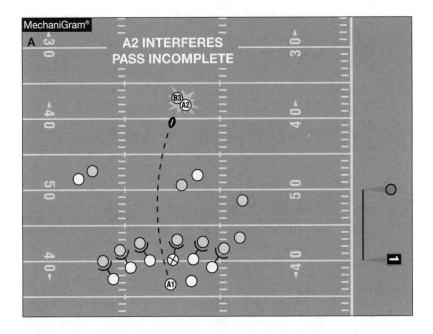

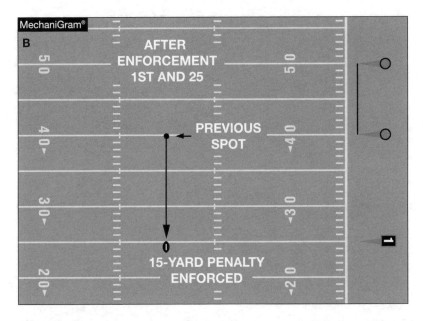

7-5-10 Penalty The loss of down portion of the penalty for offensive pass interference has been removed. When A commits pass interference (MechaniGram A), the down is replayed after enforcement of a 15-yard penalty from the previous spot (MechaniGram B).

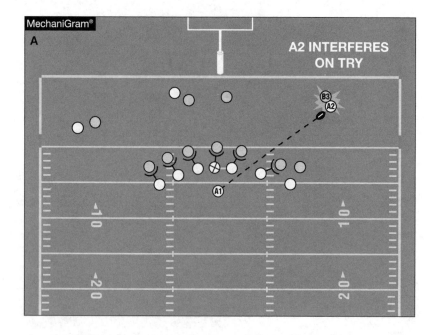

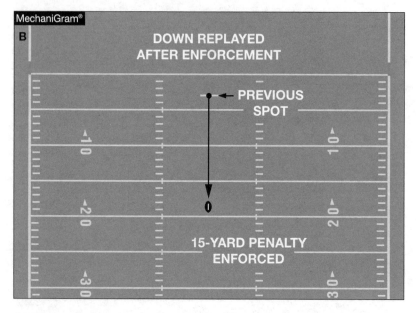

7-5-10 Penalty The loss of down portion of the penalty for offensive pass interference has been removed. When A commits pass interference on a successful try (MechaniGram A), the down is replayed after enforcement of a 15-yard penalty from the previous spot (MechaniGram B).

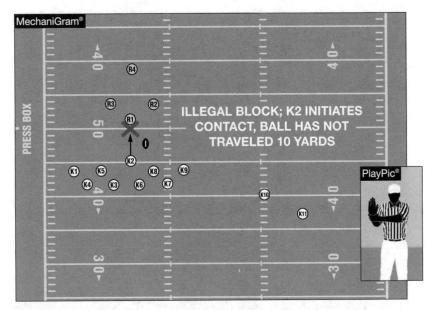

9-3-8c (New) No member of the kicking team shall initiate contact to (block) an opponent until the legal kick has traveled 10 yards; or the kicking team is eligible to recover a free-kicked ball. The signal for illegal blocks is seen in the inset.

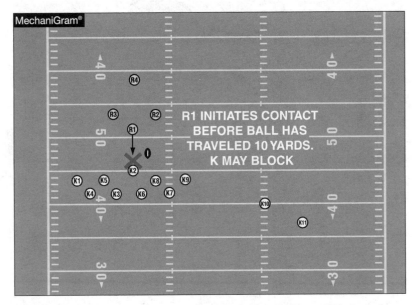

9-3-8c (New) Because R1 has initiated contact with a K player, all K players may block.

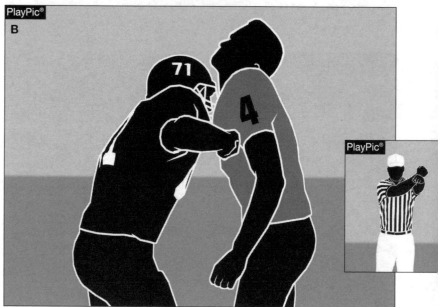

9-4-3l It is a personal foul if a player or nonplayer initiates contact with an opposing player whose helmet has come completely off.

9-6-4g If a player whose helmet comes completely off during a down continues to participate beyond the immediate action in which the player is engaged, it is a foul for illegal participation.

Part 2

2013 NFHS Points of Emphasis

Prohibition On Contact To and With the Helmet

In an effort to minimize the risk of catastrophic head and neck injuries, the NFHS Football Rules Committee continues to urge KEEPING THE HEAD OUT OF FOOTBALL. While the wearing of a football helmet can never guarantee the elimination of head and neck injuries, all levels of football have increased their focus on reducing these types of injuries as much as possible. It is recognized that one of the biggest steps in that endeavor is to eliminate direct helmet-to-helmet contact and any other contact both with and to the helmet.

Direct helmet-to-helmet contact and any other contact both with and to the helmet must be eliminated from the sport of football at the interscholastic level! Using the helmet to inflict punishment on the opponent is dangerous and illegal. Coaches and game officials must be diligent in promoting the elimination of contact to and with the helmet, as follows:

• Coaches — through consistent adherence to proper and legal coaching techniques.

• Game Officials — through strict enforcement of pertinent playing rules and game administrations.

Coaches must insist that players play "heads-up" football by utilizing proper and safe techniques — not only during games, but on the practice field as well. Coaches must shoulder the responsibility of consistently reinforcing with their players that using the top or face of the helmet goes against all tenets of the basic techniques of safe and legal blocking and tackling.

The No. 1 responsibility for game officials must be player safety. Any initiation of contact with the helmet is illegal; therefore, it must be penalized consistently and without warning. Player safety is really a matter of attitude, technique, attention and supervision. Football players will perform as they are taught; therefore, there must be a concentrated focus on consistently enforcing the existing rules. And contrary to most other rule enforcements, when in doubt, contact to and with the helmet should be ruled as a foul by game officials. Contact to and with the helmet may be considered a flagrant act and may be penalized by disqualification if a game official considers the foul so severe or extreme that it places an opponent in danger of serious injury.

Consistent education, recognition and penalty enforcement of contact to and with the helmet must be adhered to throughout practice time and contests, regardless of the situation. Whether it is in the first practice, last practice, first quarter of the first game or overtime of the state championship, contact to and with the helmet must be discouraged and taken out of the game by coaches, players and game officials. It is hoped that this concentrated approach will be a positive step toward reinforcing player safety!

Reconditioning and Recertification of Football Equipment

When addressing overall player safety related to the game of football, an essential component is the recertification and reconditioning of equipment. No piece of equipment lasts for a lifetime, but schools can safely extend the life of equipment if they follow proper procedures and guidelines before, during and after the season concludes. It is important that the equipment manager (i.e., athletic director, coach or volunteer) has a system in place to document equipment use by players, as well as recertification and/or reconditioning dates. This information serves as a valuable resource in determining future equipment needs and expenditures while providing a historical record that can be accessed if necessary.

Careful investigation should be made prior to selecting a recertification and/or reconditioning company. Quality companies will be able to guarantee that any work performed on equipment will meet national safety standards and will most likely have some type of warranty replacement program as part of the process. Schools need to protect themselves and the participants — the company the school selects should be able to provide a certificate of product liability insurance that outlines coverage limits. It is recommended that the school perform a complete evaluation of the certificate prior to entering into any agreement.

Recertification and/or reconditioning efforts are not limited to helmets. Shoulder, rib, hip, thigh, knee, tailbone and back pads need to be cleaned, sanitized and repaired each year. The company the school selects should be able to outline the recertification and/or reconditioning process that will be used and whether or not replacement parts are the manufacturer's original or from another source. Other items, such as football field equipment that utilizes padding of any type, should be inspected and repaired as well.

Minimizing risk in a football program should involve a comprehensive review of every aspect from player equipment to on-field equipment. Take the time to select a recertification and/or reconditioning company that has a proven track record with multiple clients. It is appropriate to check references before making a final selection. Recertification and/or reconditioning of equipment is an essential part of any football program. Creating a historical tracking record for equipment, repairing equipment to factory standards and recertifying equipment to meet national standards are expected. The following is some specific football reconditioning and recertification information for football helmets:

Definition of Reconditioning and Recertification

Reconditioning – The inspection, cleaning, sanitizing and repair/ restoration of athletic equipment to the original performance standard.

Recertification – The reconditioning, testing and proper labeling of athletic equipment that has previously met the NOCSAE standard and recertification standard.

What is the recommendation on how often football helmets should be reconditioned/recertified?

The helmet manufacturers recommend every year and a minimum of every other year to maintain the warranty on their helmets. The National Operating Committee on Standards for Athletic Equipment (NOCSAE) and the National Athletic Equipment Reconditioners Association (NAERA) both recommend every year. All NAERA members are licensed by NOCSAE to recondition and recertify all football helmets manufactured under the NOCSAE logo.

How often are football helmets required to be reconditioned/recertified?

The state of California is the only state that requires helmet reconditioning/recertification. The NOCSAE standards do not specify or require reconditioning or recertification of football helmets on any particular schedule or frequency. A common practice is to inspect all football helmets at the end of the football season, and schedule half of a school's inventory to be reconditioned/recertified annually. Inspection of all football helmets may identify helmets that are in need of reconditioning/recertification after each season. As of the 2012 football season, NAERA members do not recondition/recertify any helmet 10 years of age or older.

Can a football helmet be recertified without being reconditioned?

No. All helmets taken in to a NAERA facility are required to be reconditioned and recertified. A random sample of football helmets is NOCSAE drop-tested before and after the reconditioning process with the data collected on those test helmets.

Free Blocking Zone Enforcement — Consistent Enforcement of Blocking Below the Waist

The free blocking zone is defined as a rectangular area extending laterally 4 yards either side of the spot of the snap and 3 yards behind each line of scrimmage. A player is considered to be in the free-blocking zone when any part of his body is in the zone at the snap. The definition of the line of scrimmage for each team is a vertical plane through the point of the ball nearest to the team's goal line.

Blocking Below the Waist is Permitted in the Free-Blocking Zone:
1. All players involved in blocking are on the line of scrimmage and in the zone at the snap.

2. The contact is in the free-blocking zone.

3. The ball has not left the free-blocking zone.

Clipping and Blocking in the Back is Permitted in the Free-Blocking Zone:
1. By offensive linemen who are on the line of scrimmage and in the free-blocking zone at the snap.

2. Against defensive linemen who are on the line of scrimmage and in the free-blocking zone at the snap.

3. The contact is in the free-blocking zone.

4. The ball has not left the free-blocking zone.

The basic guideline is that the free-blocking zone exists while the ball is in the zone and ceases to exist when the ball has left the zone. The exception for a player to block below the waist and/or the exception for an offensive player to clip and/or block is not to continue after the ball has left the zone. With the creation of the "shotgun" and "pistol" formations, an interpretation of the free-blocking zone rule allows for an offensive lineman to legally initiate contact, immediately at the snap, with a defensive lineman by blocking below the waist, clipping or blocking in the back, even though the ball leaves the free-blocking zone soon after the snap. Any delay in the block would make it illegal, as the free-blocking zone no longer exists.

The Basic Rules to Keep in Mind at the Snap:
1. Defensive players may not clip.

2. Offensive backs may not clip.

3. Offensive linemen not in the zone at the snap may not clip.

Items for Game Officials to Consider:
1. Because a quarterback in the "shotgun" or "pistol" formation is usually positioned more than 3 yards behind the line of scrimmage at the snap, a legal block below the waist, clip or block in the back must be initiated simultaneously with the snap. Once the ball leaves the free-blocking zone, a block below the waist, clip or block in the back is a foul.

2. Offensive linemen set in a 2-point stance in a "shotgun" or "pistol" formation are particularly suspect. Any delay in executing a block below the waist, clip or block in the back after the snap in these formations results in a foul.

3. Be alert to running backs and wide receivers who line up outside the free-blocking zone, being "cut" by defenders on sweeps or roll-out passes. Blocking-below-the-waist rules apply equally to the offense and defense.

4. Up backs should not be allowed to block defenders below the waisen the team is in a scrimmage kick, shotgun or pistol formation. Only those players on the line of scrimmage and in the free-blocking zone at the time of the snap can block below the waist, and only in the free-blocking zone, and only if the free-blocking zone still exists.

Part 3
Rule 1

The Game, Field, Players and Equipment

The origin of the game of football is not clear. Football, as played in the United States, is a blend of soccer and rugby, with other variations making it a truly unique sport. Football is played with an inflated ball by two teams of 11 players each on a rectangular field 360 by 160 feet. The specific lines and marks are found on the Official NFHS Field Diagram.

Player equipment has a double purpose. It must protect the wearer and also other players against the dangers of unnecessary injury. The rules are constantly reviewed and often revised to allow use of new equipment which has been developed to provide greater protection to the participants. It is the responsibility of the rules committee to specify equipment to protect players whether on offense or defense. Because past rules committees have met this responsibility, there has been a continuous improvement in football player equipment.

The game is administered by game officials whose duties are outlined in the NFHS Football Rules Book and NFHS Football Game Officials Manual. Game officials must accept the responsibility of enforcing the letter, as well as the spirit, of the rules promptly and consistently. The safety of players is paramount and with this there can be no compromise. A thorough study and understanding of all the NFHS football publications is necessary to meet this responsibility.

1-1-7,8 The game officials' jurisdiction extends through the referee's declaration of the end of the fourth period or overtime. The game officials retain clerical authority over the game through the completion of any reports, including those imposing disqualifications, that are responsive to actions occurring while the game officials had jurisdiction. State Associations may intercede in the event of unusual incidents that occur before, during or after the game officials' jurisdiction has ended or in the event that a game is terminated prior to the conclusion of regulation play.

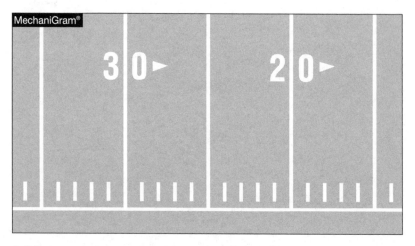

1-2-3a Lines shall be marked with a noncaustic, nontoxic material designed for marking fields such as powdered gypsum, calcium carbonate and liquid aerosol paint. It is recommended that these lines be white.

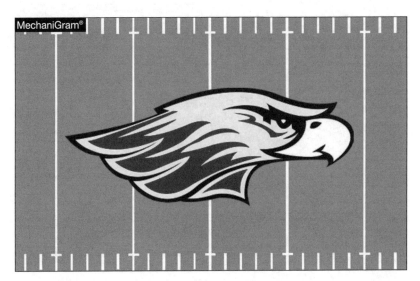

1-2-3b NOTE 2 If the field of play has a logo in the center or at any other part of the field of play, that logo shall not obstruct the visibility of the required marks every five yards. This logo would not be legal and should be reported to the state association after the game.

1-2-3b NOTE 2 A solid or shadow-bordered 4-inch wide line is permissible A shadow line is a line that designates the required 4-inch width by use of a border or outline lines at least 1/4-inch wide, which shall lie within the 4-inch width. Shadow lines that are the natural color of the field of play are permissible. The area within these lines need not be one color, but the continuous 4-inch wide outline must be clearly visible to the game officials.

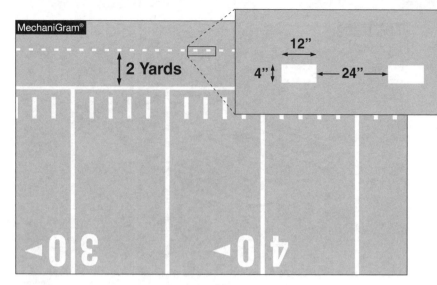

1-2-3d It is recommended that the restraining line be marked by placing 12-inch-long lines, separated at 24-inch intervals.

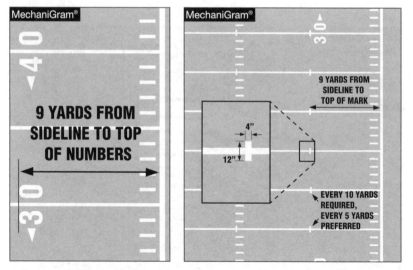

1-2-3f 9-yard marks or numbers are required for all fields.

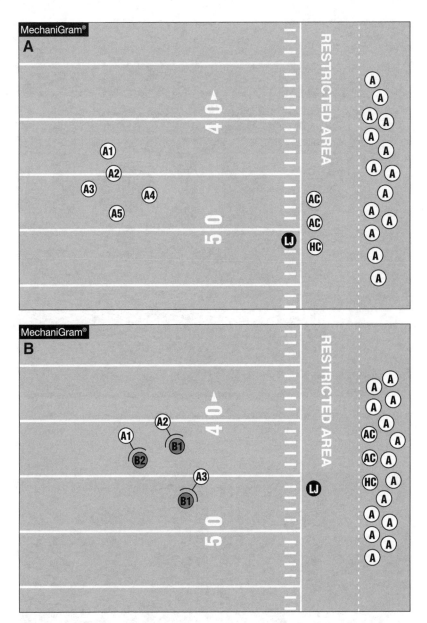

1-2-3g, 9-8-3 When the ball is dead, a maximum of three coaches may be in the restricted area (A). Once the ball is snapped, no nonplayer may be in the restricted area (B). The first offense is results in a team warning; the second offense, a five-yard penalty for sideline interference; and subsequent offenses, 15 yards for unsportsmanlike conduct charged to the head coach. The two-yard restricted area may only be used when the ball is dead.

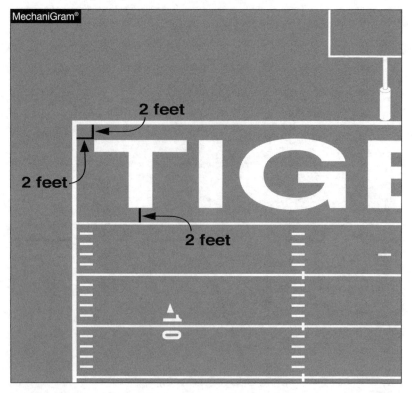

1-2-3h Decorative markings in the end zones shall be no closer than 2 feet from the boundary and the goal lines.

1-2-3I Advertising and/or commercial markings may not obstruct the yard lines, hash marks or 9-yard marks. The logo in MechaniGram A is illegal, but the one in MechaniGram B is legal.

1-3-1c A legal football has a continuous 1-inch white or yellow stripe centered 3 to 3-1/4 inches from each end of the ball free from decorations or logos added during or after production. The stripes shall be located only on the two panels adjacent to the laces (A). Footballs with acontinuous solid white or yellow stripes 3/8 inch wide running parallel to and 1/4 inch from each side of each seam to 1 inch from the laces (B) are not allowed.

1-3-2 It is permissible for either team to have an additional ball(s) approved during the course of the game. When weather conditions change it is often necessary to use a different ball. In normal situations the referee will approve and mark the balls before game time.

"HOLDING"

1-3-7 State associations may authorize use of supplementary equipment to aid in game administration. The microphone on the referee and the 25-second field clock are just two examples of equipment which can be used when properly authorized.

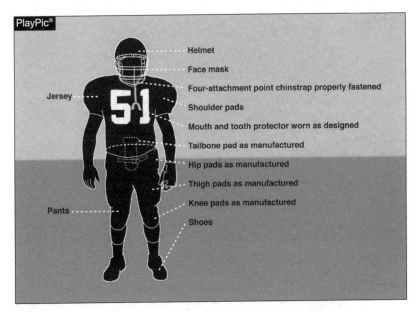

1-5-1 The items of equipment shown must be worn by all players A player may not participate unless he or she is wearing all required equipment which is professionally manufactured and not altered to decrease protection .

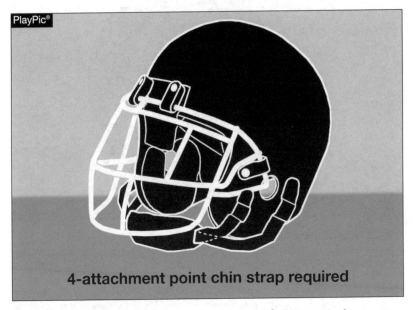

4-attachment point chin strap required

1-5-1a2 At least a four-attachment point chin strap shall be required to secure the helmet.

1-5-1a Note A visible, exterior warning label is required on each player's helmet. The warning label is a statement concerning the risk of injury. The coach's pregame verification to the referee and umpire that all players are equipped in compliance with the rules includes the exterior warning label.

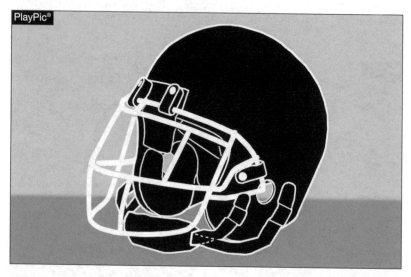

1-5-1a, Note A face mask which met the NOCSAE* test standard at the time of manufacture is required. The face mask shall be made of material designed to be nonbreakable with rounded edges, and those constructed of metal shall have the surface covered with resilient material designed to prevent chipping, burrs or abrasiveness which would endanger players. The face mask shall be properly secured to a helmet which met the NOCSAE test standard at the time of manufacture and has a visible exterior warning label regarding the risk of injury.
*National Operating Committee on Standards for Athletic Equipment.

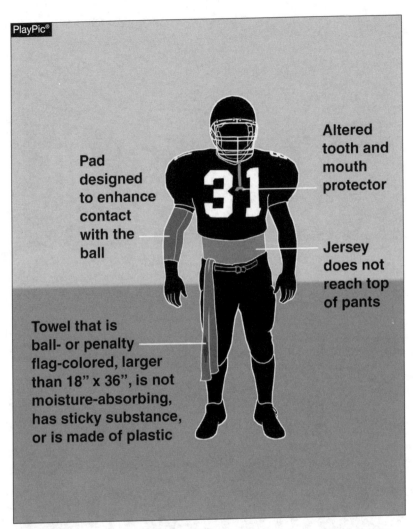

Pad designed to enhance contact with the ball

Altered tooth and mouth protector

Jersey does not reach top of pants

Towel that is ball- or penalty flag-colored, larger than 18" x 36", is not moisture-absorbing, has sticky substance, or is made of plastic

1-5-1b(1); 1-5-3a(5)a, 1-5-3c(5), 1-5-3c(9) No player may participate while wearing illegal equipment, an illegal uniform or with equipment that has been illegally altered.

1-5-1c These jersey numerals are legal. Different styles of numerals also are legal as long as they are Arabic numbers 1 through 99 and they are clearly visible and legible. All players of one team must wear numbers identical in style front and back and no teammates may participate wearing identical numbers.

1-5-1c(1), 1-5-1c(2) The number on each jersey shall be clearly visible and legible. The jersey on the left is illegal because the number shall also be centered on the jersey horizontally, as in the jersey on the right.

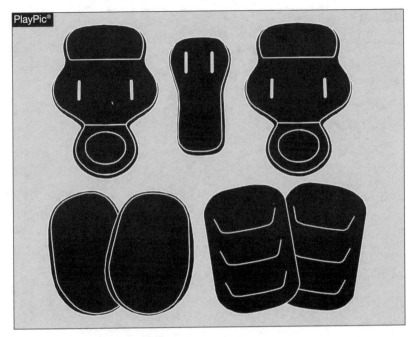

1-5-1d(1), 1-5-1d(2), 1-5-1d(4) Hip pads and tailbone protector, knee pads, and thigh guards must be unaltered from the manufacturer's original design/production.

1-5-1d(5) A tooth and mouth protector (intraoral) which shall include an occlusal (protecting and separating the biting surfaces) and a labial (protecting the teeth and supporting structures) portion and covers the posterior teeth with adequate thickness is required. It is recommended the protector be properly fitted and constructed from a model made from an impression of the individual's teeth and constructed and fitted to the individual by impressing the teeth into the tooth and mouth protector itself.

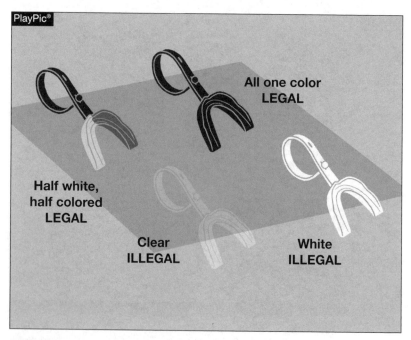

1-5-1d(5) Tooth and mouth protectors shall be of any readily visible color, other than completely white or completely clear.

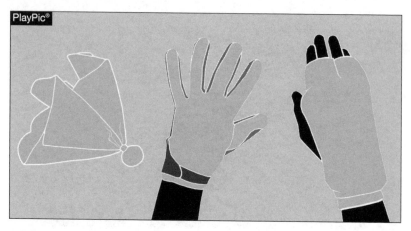

1-5-2b Gloves and hand pads may be the same color as penalty markers.

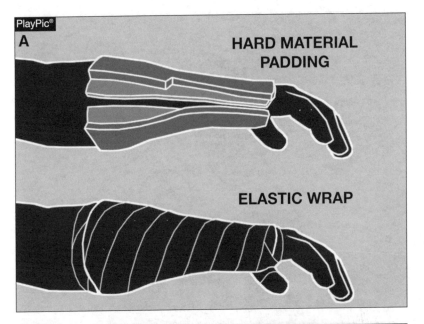

HARD MATERIAL PADDING

ELASTIC WRAP

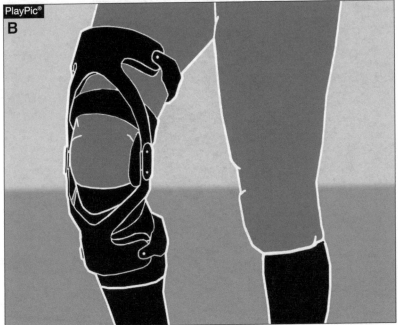

1-5-3b(1), 1-5-3b(3) Hard and unyielding items (guards, casts, braces, etc.) on the hand, wrist, forearm, elbow, or upper arm (A) must be padded with a closed-cell, slow-recovery foam padding no less than one-half inch in thickness. Knee braces may not be worn on top of the pants (B).

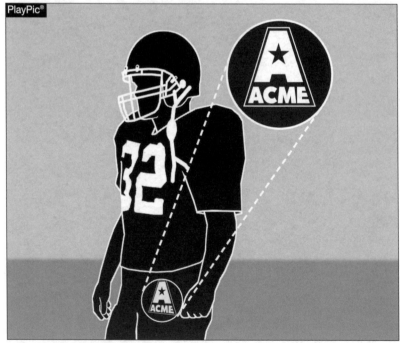

1-5-3a(1)a, 1-5-3a(1)b Jerseys/pants may have only one reference to the manufacturer and the reference on each may not exceed 2-1/4 square inches. The references shown are too large and would be illegal.

1-5-3c(8) If worn, play cards must be worn on the wrist or arm, as seen in PlayPic A. Play cards may not be attached to the belt (PlayPic B) or otherwise worn.

1-5-3c(3) If worn, eye shade (grease or no-glare strips or stickers) that is not a solid stroke or includes words, numbers, logos or other symbols within the eye shade is illegal. If a player uses eye shade, it must be applied using a single solid stroke under each eye. The eye shade shall be located below and within the width of the eye socket and not extend below the cheek bone.

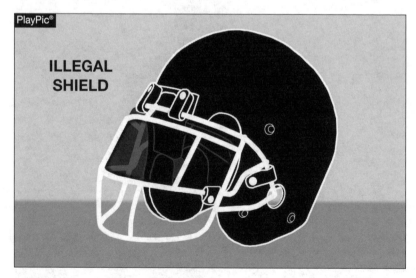

1-5-3c(4) If an eyeshield is worn, it must be constructed of a molded, rigid material that is clear without the presence of any tint.

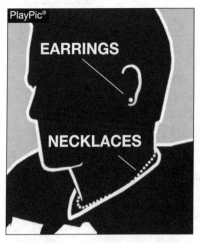

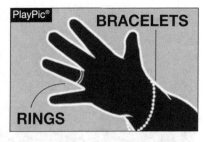

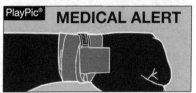

1-5-3c(6) Jewelry such as earrings, necklaces, bracelets and rings shall not be worn. Religious and medical-alert medals are not considered jewelry. A religious medal must be taped and worn under the uniform. A medical-alert medal must be taped and may be visible.

1-5-4 Prior to the game, the referee and umpire must visit each team. The head coach is responsible for verifying to the referee in the presence of the umpire that all his players are legally equipped and in compliance with the rules. The umpire will examine and determine legality of any questionable player equipment.

1-6-2 LAN phones and/or headsets may be used by coaches, other nonplayers and players; however, players may use LAN phones and/or headsets only during authorized outside 9-yard mark conferences.

1-6-2 An authorized conference in front of the team box can be conducted as far onto the field as the 9-yard marks. Regardless if the conference takes place between the hash marks or within the 9-yard marks in front of the team box, a coach may use LAN phones or headphones.

1-7 Each state association may, in keeping with applicable laws, authorize exceptions to NFHS playing rules to provide reasonable accommodations to individual participants with disabilities and/or special needs, as well as those individuals with unique and extenuating circumstances. The accommodations should not fundamentally alter the sport or heighten risk to the athlete/others or place opponents at a disadvantage.

Rule 2

Definitions of Playing Terms

Coaches and game officials have a tendency to overlook Rule 2, thinking that definitions are not as important as, for example, those situations dealing with various types of rules infractions and their respective penalties. Nothing could be further from the truth. Rule 2, indeed, is the most important rule in the book. A few examples of some basic definitions:

1. Batting is intentionally slapping or striking the ball with the arm or hand.
2. A catch is the act of establishing player possession of a live ball in flight.
3. Force is not a factor when a backward pass or fumble is declared dead in the end zone of the opponent of the player who passed or fumbled, with no player possession.
4. A fumble is any loss of player possession other than by legal kick, passing or handing.
5. The line of scrimmage for each team is a vertical plane through the point of the ball nearest the team's goal line.
6. The neutral zone is the space between the two free-kick lines during a free-kick down and between the two scrimmage lines during a scrimmage down.

A–refers to the offensive team that puts the ball in play during a scrimmage down. B–refers to their opponents, the defensive team. K–refers to the kicking team, while R–identifies the receiving team during a free or scrimmage kick. The offense is the team which is in possession. At such time, the opponent is the defense.

To fully understand the game, everyone concerned must have a complete understanding of the definitions. The definitions are clear and concise. Terms used in the definitions are unique and actually form the language of the game.

2-3-2a This is a legal blocking position with closed or cupped hands. The hands are in advance of the elbows and not extended more than 45 degrees from the body. The elbows may be either inside or outside the frame of the shoulders. The hands are closed or cupped with the palms not facing the opponents. The forearms may not be extended more than 45 degrees from the blocker's body. If they are, the hands must be open and shall not be locked.

2-3-2b This is a legal blocking position with extended arms and open hands. Team A blockers may use open hands when blocking if the hands are in advance of the elbows and within the blocker's frame and the opponent's frame. The hands must be open when the forearms are extended more than 45 degrees from the blocker's body.

  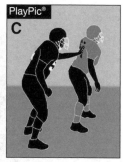

2-3-2b, 2-5-2 The PlayPics depict contact outside the free-blocking zone. The original contact in (A) is legal (2-5-2). However, the opponent evades the blocker in (B). The blocker makes illegal contact on the back in (C). The block was not continuous and results in a block in the back foul in (C). If the blocker had maintained contact in (B) the block would have been legal.

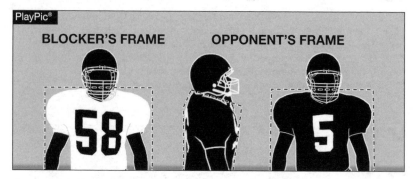

2-3-2b (2 & 3) The frame of the blocker's body is the front of the body at or below the shoulders. The frame of the opponent's body is at the shoulders or below, other than the back.

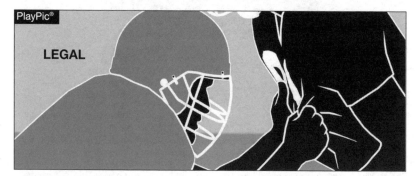

2-3-5b Any defensive player (shown in gray) may use hands to get to a runner or loose ball as long as such contact is not pass interference, a personal foul or illegal use of hands.

2-3-7 Contact with an opponent's hand(s) above the waist (PlayPic A) that continues into the body below the waist (PlayPic B) is legal.

2-3-7 Contact with an opponent's hand(s) below the waist (PlayPic A) that continues into the body below the waist (PlayPic B) is considered blocking below the waist.

2-3-8, 9-3-6 Table A chop block is a combination block by two or more teammates against an opponent other than the runner, with or without delay, where one of the blocks is low (at the knee or below) and one of the blocks is high (above the knee).

2-3-8, 9-3-6 Table Combination blocks in the free-blocking zone that consist of either two low blocks (at the knee or below) or two high blocks are legal .

2-4-1 No catch. The receiver does not have possession of the ball inbounds when he comes down. When there is possession, the first foot to touch the ground determines whether it is a catch — as it must touch inbounds, even if the other foot then touches out of bounds. If the feet touch the ground simultaneously, both must be inbounds.

2-4-1 A catch is the act of establishing player possession of a live ball which is in flight, and first contacting the ground inbounds while maintaining possession of the ball. Because the player's foot is inbounds when he grasps the ball (PlayPic A), and maintains possession after the contact and landing out of bounds (PlayPic B), it is a catch.

2-4-1 The airborne player grasps the ball (PlayPic A), but after the contact by an opponent (PlayPic B), he lands out of bounds (PlayPic C). That is not a catch.

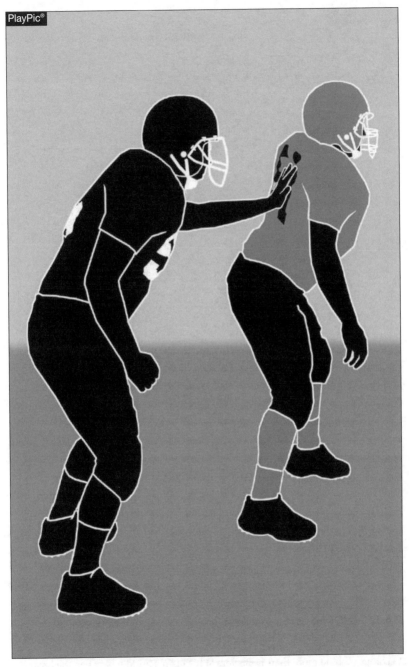

2-5-2 Blocking in the back is against an opponent with the initial contact inside the shoulders, below the helmet and above the waist. The penalty for blocking in the back is 10 yards.

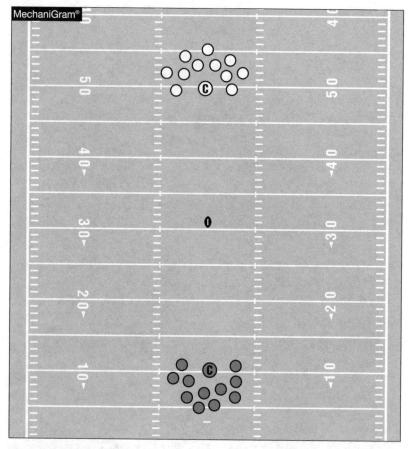

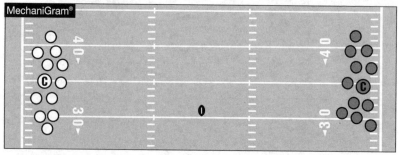

2-6-1, 2-6-2 When a team's request for a charged team time-out is granted, the teams shall use of two types of authorized team conferences. The "between 9-yard mark conferences" (MechaniGram A) involve one coach on the field to confer with no more than 11 players at his team's huddle between the hash marks. The "outside 9-yard mark conference" (MechaniGram B) consists of one or more team members and one or more coaches directly in front of the team box within 9 yards of the sideline.

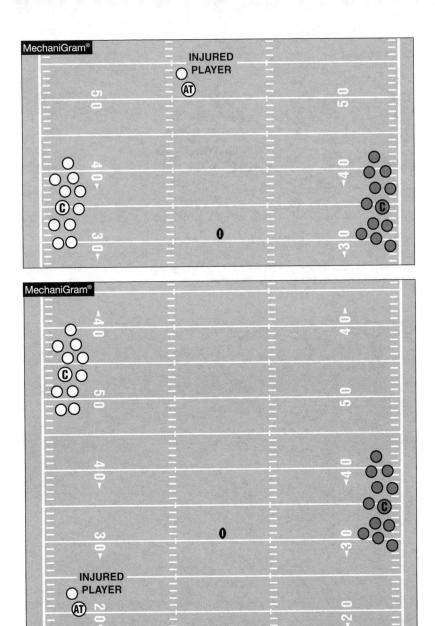

2-6-1, 2-6-2 When an injury occurs and the referee grants an authorized conference, it must be an "outside 9-yard mark conference" (MechaniGram A). If the injured player is outside the 9-yard marks but in front of the team box, the conference must still be conducted outside the 9-yard marks and in front of the restricted area but away from the injured player (MechaniGram B). That will give medical personnel time and space to address the injured player.

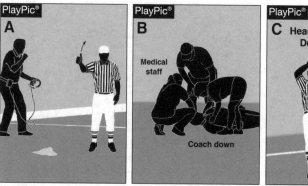

2-6-2a, 3-5-2a, 3-5-2a Note If the head coach is not on the sideline, such as due to a disqualification (A) or injury (B), the head coach may designate someone to request time-outs from the sideline (C). The designee shall remain in place for the entire game except in case of emergency.

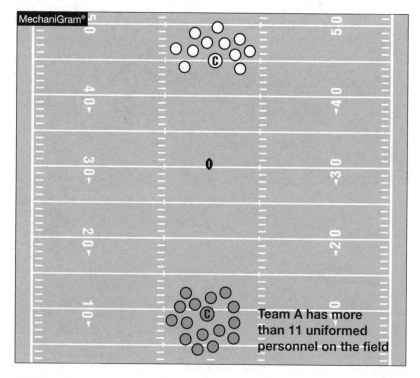

Team A has more than 11 uniformed personnel on the field

2-6-2b It is illegal to have more than 11 players meet with the coach for a conference between the hash marks. The penalty is 15 yards (9-8-1f).

2-9-1 The prohibition against contacting a player who has given a valid fair-catch signal ceases if the kick is muffed. When No. 80 catches the ball in (D), it is a fair catch. The contact in (C) is ignored unless unnecessarily rough or flagrant. The captain may choose to snap or free kick anywhere between the hash marks on the yard line through the spot of the catch.

2-9-4 A signal given after the kick has touched a receiver or after it has touched the ground is an invalid fair-catch signal. The ball becomes dead as soon as the kick is caught or recovered. The foul will be enforced as a post-scrimmage kick foul.

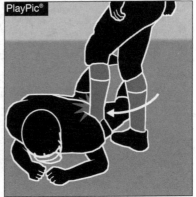

2-11 Fighting is any attempt by a player or nonplayer to strike or engage a player or nonplayer in a combative manner unrelated to football. Included are attempts to strike with hand(s), arm(s), leg(s), feet or foot, whether or not there is contact. The four examples of fighting pictured all call for a 15-yard penalty and disqualification.

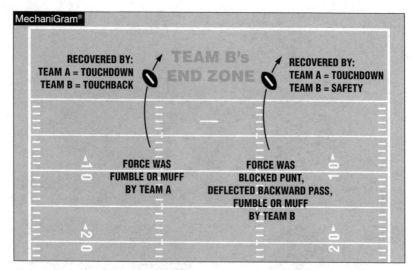

2-13-1 Force is the result of energy exerted by a player which provides movement of the ball. A new force may result from a fumble, kick or backward pass which has been grounded. Force is a factor only when it concerns the goal line and in only one direction — from the field of play into the end zone. On kicks going into R's end zone, force is not a factor since it is a touchback regardless of who supplied the force.

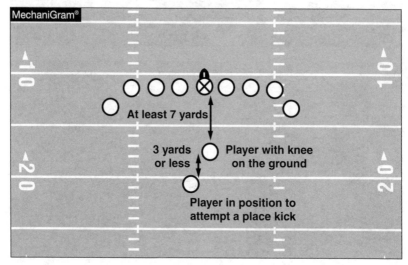

2-14-2a Legal scrimmage-kick formation. The kicking team has a player in position with a knee on the ground 7 or more yards behind the line of scrimmage, in position to be the holder and in position to receive the long snap and with another player three yards or less behind the holder in position to attempt a place kick.

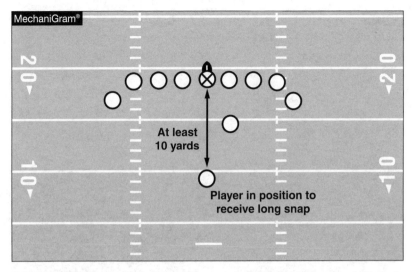

2-14-2b Legal scrimmage-kick formation. A member of the kicking team is 10 yards or more behind the line of scrimmage and in position to receive the long snap.

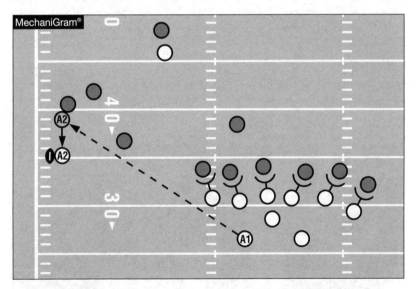

2-15-2 The airborne receiver possesses the pass at the 39-yard line. The defensive contact causes him to be driven backward and the catch is completed well short of the 39 Since the defender caused the change in direction, forward progress is awarded to the farthest advancement after possessing the ball.

2-15-2 Airborne receiver No. 5 possesses the ball beyond the plane of B's goal line. The defensive contact forces No. 5 out of the end zone and the catch is completed in the field of play No. 5 is given forward progress at the point of possession and it is a touchdown.

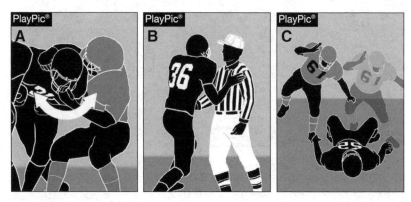

2-16-2c Any single flagrant foul results in disqualification of the offender. Among the acts that may be considered flagrant are violent and repeated pulls on a face mask (A), intentional contact of a game official (B) and prolonged taunting of an opponent (C).

2-16-2e, 10-2-4 It is a multiple foul when two or more live-ball fouls (other than nonplayer or unsportsmanlike) are committed during the same down by the same team (A). One penalty must be declined (B) as only one may be enforced (C).

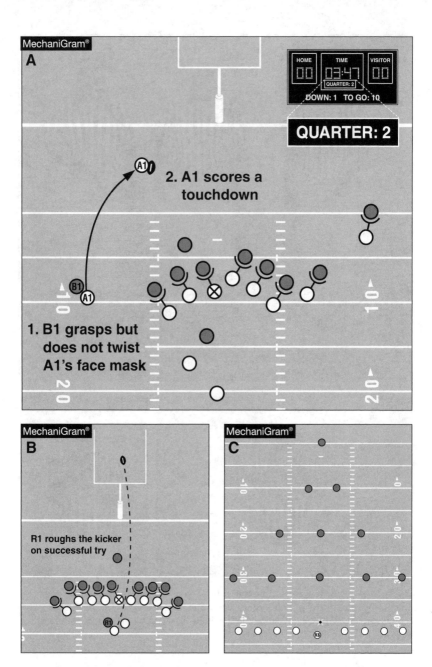

2-16-2e, 8-2-2, 8-2-3, 10-2-4 The opponent of the scoring team commits a live-ball foul (other than unsportmanlike conduct or a nonplayer foul) during a down in which there was no change of possession (A). The same team commits a live-ball foul during the try (B). Both penalties may be enforced on the subsequent kickoff (C).

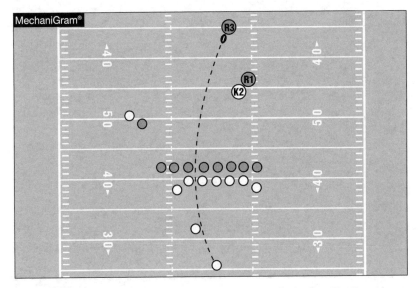

2-16-2h During the scrimmage kick, R1 blocks K2 in the back at R's 45-yard line. The post-scrimmage kick spot is the end of the kick, which is R's 35-yard line.

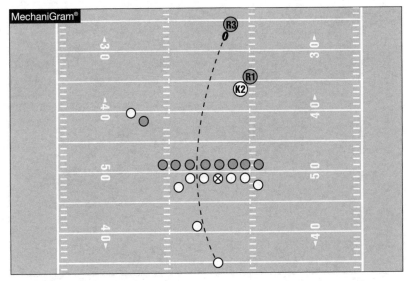

2-16-2h During the scrimmage kick, K2 grasps R1's face mask at R's 35-yard line as R3 makes a fair catch. The post-scrimmage kick enforcement procedure does not apply on K fouls. This penalty is enforced from the previous spot.

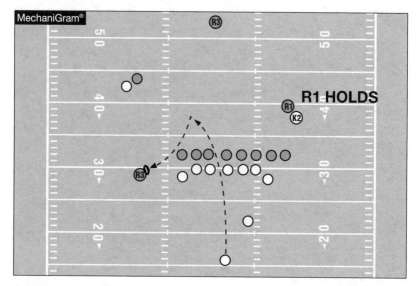

2-16-2h R1 holds during the kick, which is recovered by R3 behind the line. The penalty is enforced from the spot of the foul as this is behind the PSK spot.

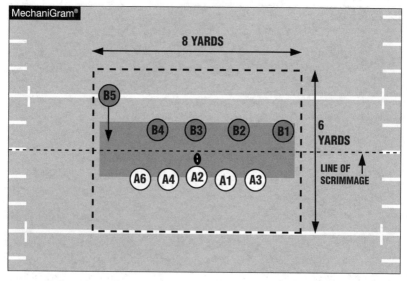

2-17-2 In 11-player football, all players involved in blocking below the waist must be on the line of scrimmage and in the free-blocking zone at snap. Also, the contact must take place in the zone. B5 moves to line of scrimmage just prior to the ball being snapped and therefore meets the definition of a lineman.

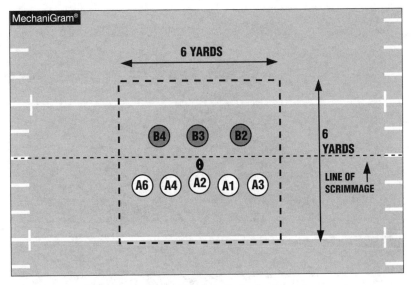

2-17-2 In nine- eight- and six-player football, the free-blocking zone is a square area extending laterally 3 yards either side of the spot of the snap and 3 yards behind each line of scrimmage.

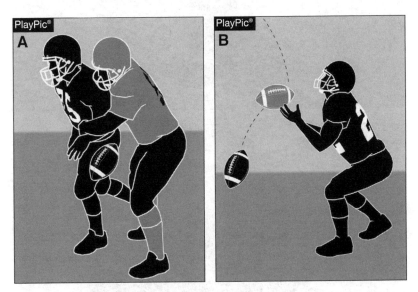

2-18 A fumble (A) is any loss of player possession other than by kick, pass or handing. A fumble may be recovered and advanced by any player of either team. A muff (B) occurs when a player touches a loose ball in an unsuccessful attempt to gain possession.

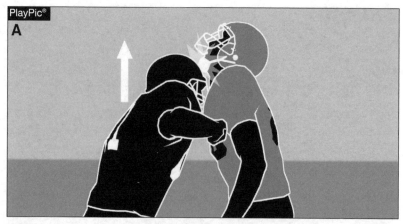

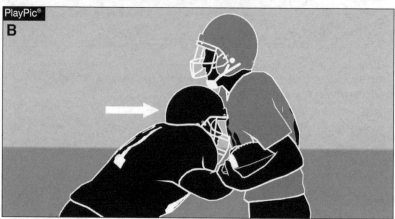

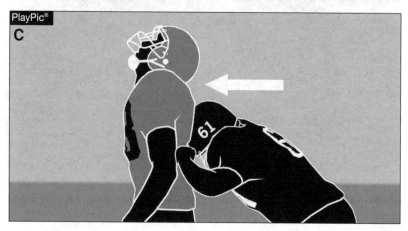

2-20, 9-4-3i, 9-4-3i Note Illegal helmet contact is dangerous. Butt blocking (A), face tackling (B) and spearing (C) are all fouls carrying a 15-yard penalty.

2-20-1c No. 61 is spearing. If the contact is of such severity that it is ruled flagrant, the offender shall be disqualified. The use of the helmet to punish and abuse an opponent cannot be tolerated and the rule declaring it illegal must be strictly enforced.

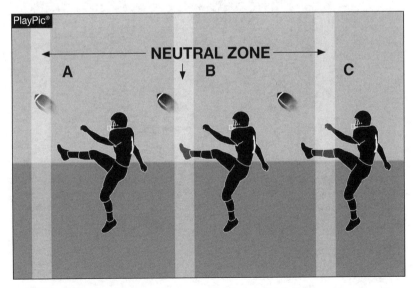

2-24-4 A legal scrimmage kick is made from in or behind the neutral zone as in (A) and (B). As in a forward-pass play, the down marker can be used as a reference point because it denotes the forward limit of the neutral zone. In (C) it is an illegal kick because the kicker's foot was beyond the neutral-zone plane on contact.

2-25-2 In (A) No. 88 is not on his line because neither his head or foot breaks the plane through the snapper's waist. In (B) No. 88 is legally on the line.

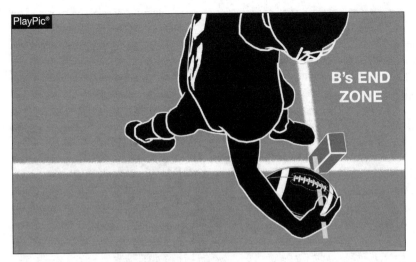

2-26-3 A touchdown is scored even though the ball has not penetrated the goal-line plane inside the sideline Since the runner is touching inbounds when the ball breaks the plane of the goal-line extended, it is a touchdown. However, if the runner is not touching inbounds when the ball breaks the plane of the goal-line extended, it is not a touchdown and the ball is spotted where it broke the sideline plane.

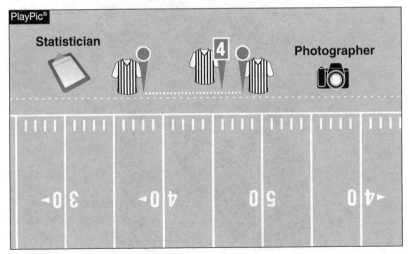

2-26-8, 9-8-3 A restraining line is a line placed around the outside of the field. No person, including but not limited to, spectators, game administrators or members of the media, shall be allowed within the restraining line. A maximum of three coaches as well as permitted nonplayers are allowed within the restraining line in front of the team box, as provided for in Rule 9-8-3, as long as the ball is dead.

2-31-2 Note The game official must rule whether the action illustrated results in a fumble or an incomplete pass. The game official is to make his judgement based upon the movement of the passer's arm at contact. If the arm is stationary or moving backward away from the line of scrimmage on contact (A), the result is a fumble. If the arm is moving forward toward the line of scrimmage on contact (B), the result is an incomplete pass.

**K MISSES BALL
R MAKES CONTACT**

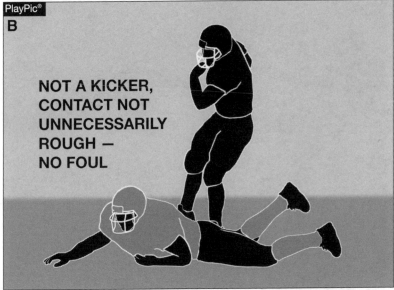

**NOT A KICKER,
CONTACT NOT
UNNECESSARILY
ROUGH —
NO FOUL**

2-32-8 A player becomes a kicker when his knee, lower leg or foot makes contact with the ball. When the player in PlayPic A "whiffs" on the kick, he is not considered a kicker. The contact by the opponent only caused the K player to lose his balance and was not unnecessarily rough (PlayPic B). There is no foul.

2-32-8 A player becomes a kicker when his knee, lower leg or foot makes contact with the ball. In (A), the K player is a runner, not a kicker. It is the defensive player's obligation by rule to avoid illegal contact. The covering official must judge if the defender had reasonable opportunity that a kick would be made.

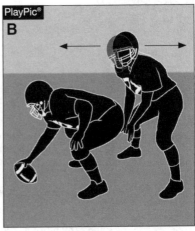

2-39 It is a shift when the quarterback goes from his position in (A) to his presnap position in (B). The movement of his head and/or shoulders in (B) is not a shift, but would be a false start if it simulated the start of a play. After assuming the position in (B), the quarterback and the other players of A must be simultaneously stationary for at least one second before the snap or before a player goes in motion.

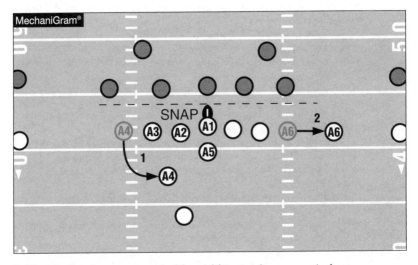

2-39 Whether the movement in (1) and (2) is simultaneous or is done individually, it is a shift. It is a shift whether the movement is to the line, from the line or along the line. The movement of one or more A players to a new position is a shift. It is also a shift when the offensive team moves from the huddle or a player(s) goes from an upright or hands-on-knees position to a down position. Following a shift, all Team A players must be simultaneously set for at least one second before the snap or before a player goes in motion.

Rule 3

Periods, Time Factors and Substitutions

The clock running time for high school football games is 48 minutes, divided into four 12-minute periods. Between the second and third periods, there is an intermission of 15 minutes followed immediately by a three-minute interval for required warm-up activity preceding the beginning of the third period. With proper notification, the intermission may be extended to a maximum of 20 minutes. The opposing coaches may agree to reduce the intermission to a minimum of 10 minutes.

Periods may be shortened in any emergency by agreement of the opposing coaches and the referee. By mutual agreement of the opposing coaches and the referee, any remaining period may be shortened at any time or the game terminated. When weather conditions are considered to be hazardous to the participants, the crew of game officials is authorized to suspend the game. An official's time-out is authorized when heat/humidity may create a health risk for players.

Obvious errors in timing may be corrected by the referee if discovery of the error is made prior to the second live ball following the error, unless the period has officially ended. No other adjustment in timing is authorized.

The rules are extremely liberal insofar as substitutions are concerned. There are seven possible violations:

1. When a substitute enters during the live-ball period.
2. When a player who has been replaced is not off the field before the ball becomes live.
3. When a substitute enters the game and is then replaced or a replaced player re-enters as a substitute during the same dead-ball period unless during that interval, there was acceptance of a penalty, a dead-ball foul, a charged time-out or the end of a period.
4. When a replaced player, or a substitute who was unable to complete a substitution does not leave the field on the side of his team box.
5. When a replaced player does not attempt to leave the field within 3 seconds.
6. When an entering substitute is not on his team's side of the neutral zone at the snap.
7. When a replaced player, player or substitute leaves the field opposite the side of his team box or over the end line.

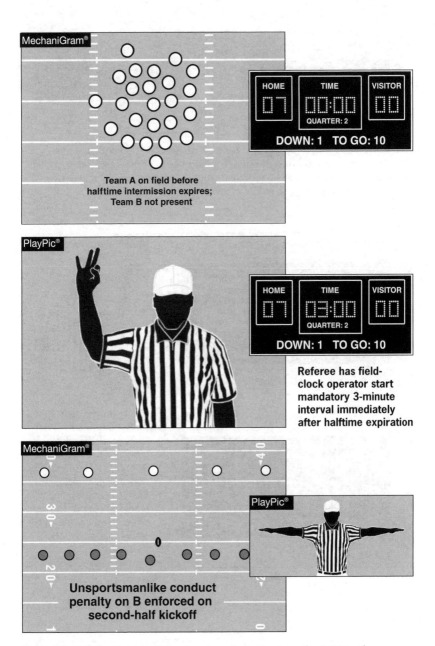

Team A on field before halftime intermission expires; Team B not present

HOME `07` TIME `00:00` QUARTER: 2 VISITOR `00`
DOWN: 1 TO GO: 10

Referee has field-clock operator start mandatory 3-minute interval immediately after halftime expiration

HOME `07` TIME `03:00` QUARTER: 2 VISITOR `00`
DOWN: 1 TO GO: 10

Unsportsmanlike conduct penalty on B enforced on second-half kickoff

Table 3-1, 9-8-1g Responsibility for a team being back on the field for the mandatory three-minute warm-up period, which begins immediately following the conclusion of the scheduled halftime intermission, rests with the head coach. An unsportsmanlike conduct penalty will be assessed to the head coach if the team is not back on the field prior to the start of the mandatory warm-up period.

	1 MINUTE BETWEEN QUARTERS		15 MINUTES BETWEEN HALVES PLUS 3 MINUTE WARM-UP		1 MINUTE BETWEEN QUARTERS	
1st QUARTER		**2nd QUARTER**		**3rd QUARTER**		**4th QUARTER**

3-1-1 The normal 15-minute period between halves may be extended by state association approval to a maximum of 20 minutes upon proper notification at least five minutes prior to scheduled kickoff. By mutual agreement of the coaches, the halftime intermission may be reduced to a minimum of 10 minutes.

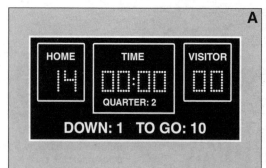

3-1-1 Immediately after the halftime intermission expires (A), the referee must signal the timer (B) to put 3 minutes on the clock (C) and to immediately start the clock for the mandatory warm-up period. The head coach is responsible for his team being on the field for the mandatory warm-up at the end of the intermission.

3-1-2, Table 1-7 (8) State associations have the option to use the running clock at any time during the game.

3-1-5 When weather conditions are determined to be hazardous to the participants, the crew of game officials is authorized to delay the start or suspend the game. Interrupted games shall be continued from the point of interruption, unless the teams agree to accept the existing score as final, or there are conference, league or state association rules which apply.

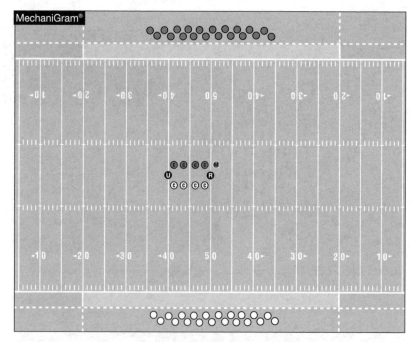

3-2-2 When the coin toss or simulated coin toss occurs three minutes before game time, not more than four team members in game uniform (captains) from each team shall be present for the coin toss. Others present at the coin toss are game management decisions in compliance with state association policy. All other team members in game uniform must remain outside the field of play.

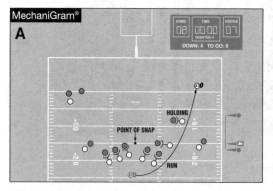

3-3-3a Since the offensive holding foul in (A) occurred during the last timed down of a period, the period will be extended with an untimed down if the penalty is accepted. If the penalty is declined, the touchdown is scored and the period is over following the try. An unsportsmanlike foul or a nonplayer foul is not considered when determining if a period is to be extended because such penalty is automatically enforced from the succeeding spot. An untimed down is indicated by using the signal in (B).

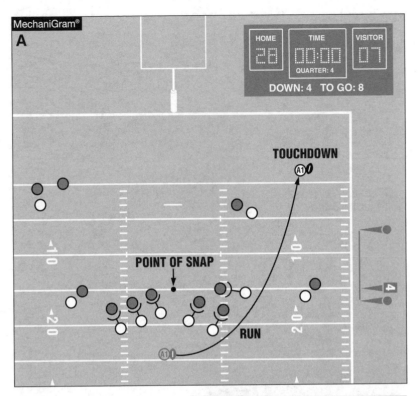

MechaniGram®

A

HOME 28 | TIME 00:00 QUARTER: 4 | VISITOR 07

DOWN: 4   TO GO: 8

TOUCHDOWN

POINT OF SNAP

RUN

3-3-3d In (A), a touchdown is scored during the last down of the fourth period. The winner of the game has already been determined. In (B) the referee gives the signal to indicate the game is ended. The try is waived unless the potential point(s) is necessary or required as part of the state association's play-off qualification system.

PlayPic®

B

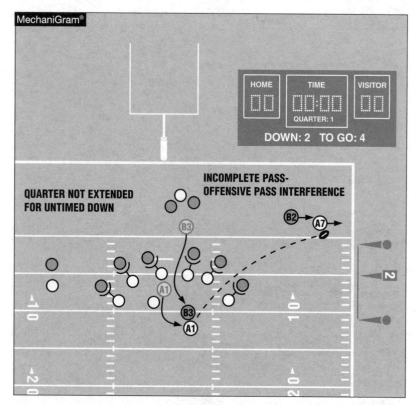

3-3-4b Offensive pass interference occurred on this incomplete pass during the last timed down of a period. The period will be not extended with an untimed down if the penalty is accepted. An unsportsmanlike foul or a nonplayer foul is not considered when determining if a period is to be extended because such penalty is enforced from the succeeding spot.,

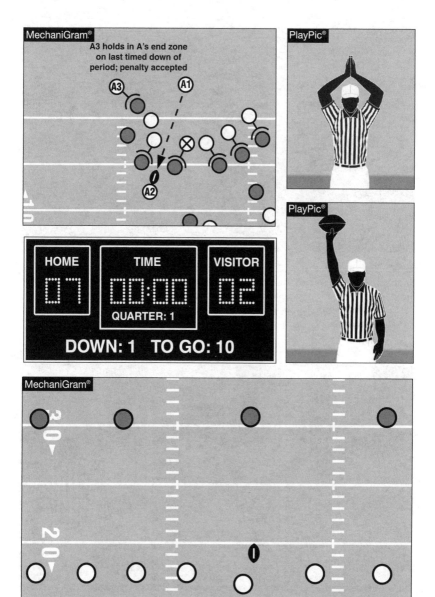

MechaniGram®

A3 holds in A's end zone on last timed down of period; penalty accepted

PlayPic®

PlayPic®

HOME	TIME	VISITOR
07	00:00	02
	QUARTER: 1	

DOWN: 1   TO GO: 10

MechaniGram®

Period not extended; teams switch ends for the free kick

3-3-4b(5) If on the last timed down of a period enforcement of an accepted penalty results in a safety, the period is not extended for the ensuing free kick. The teams change goals and the free kick is the first play of the next quarter.

3-3-5 This foul by B is a dead-ball foul. All dead-ball fouls after the end of the first half are enforced on the third period kickoff. If a dead-ball foul occurs after time has expired for any period, the penalty is measured from the succeeding spot. This succeeding spot could be the subsequent kickoff or the start of an overtime period

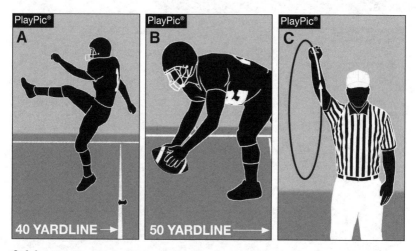

3-4-1a During a kickoff or any other free kick (A), the clock will not be started until the ball is touched, other than first touching by. K. When K touches the ball beyond the neutral zone, as in (B), the clock is started (C). When K secures possession, the ball becomes dead and the clock is stopped. K may not advance the ball. The recovery by K results in a first down for K.

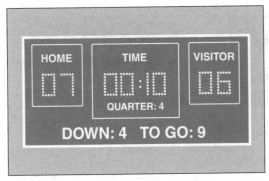

3-4-3i If the penalty is accepted for a delay-of-game foul, the clock shall start with the snap. A number of specific situations constitute delay of game, however, any conduct which unduly prolongs the game is delay.

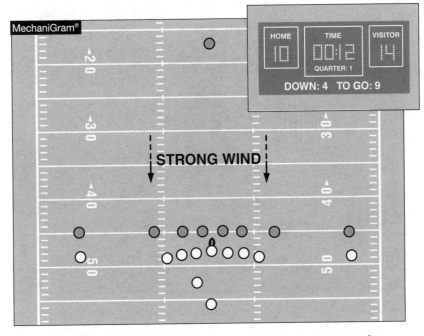

STRONG WIND

3-4-6 Whenever a team attempts to conserve or consume time illegally, the referee shall order the clock started or stopped. The kicking team tried to consume time and fouled to keep from kicking into the wind. By altering the normal timing procedure, no advantage can be gained because the clock will not start until the snap.

3-5-1 Each team is entitled to three charged team timeouts during each half. Unused first half time-outs cannot be used in the second half. Unused second half time-outs cannot be used in overtime. The visiting team had all three charged team time-outs remaining in the second half and the home team had none (A). Each team is entitled to one charged team time-out in each overtime period (B).

HEAD COACH OR HEAD COACH'S DESIGNEE

3-5-2a The head coach or the head coach's designee may request a time-out.

"ANOTHER TIME-OUT"

3-5-4 Successive charged time-outs may be granted each team during a dead-ball period provided the team has time-outs remaining. Each team is entitled to three during each half. Unused time-outs from the first half cannot be used in the second half or in overtime. Unused second half time-outs may be utilized in overtime if allowed by state association rules. No single charged time-out shall exceed one minute. When a team has used its allowable time-outs in each half, its coach and captain should be notified. A time-out may not be shortened unless both teams are ready to play.

3-5-10 It is an officials' time-out whenever a request is made for a designated injured player who is then required to leave the field for at least one down. The player must leave the game for one down, even if his team subsequently takes a charged time-out in this situation. It is illegal participation if the injured player does not stay out for at least one down unless the halftime or an overtime intermission occurs prior to the next down.

3-5-10b Any player who exhibits signs, symptoms or behaviors consistent with a concussion (such as loss of consciousness, headache, dizziness, confusion or balance problems) shall be immediately removed from the game (A) and shall not return to play until cleared by an appropriate health-care professional (B).

3-5-10c When a game official discovers any player who is bleeding, has an open wound, has any amount of blood on his/her uniform, or has blood on his/her person, he shall stop the clock or delay the ready-for-play signal. The player must leave the game for at least one down under provisions of the apparently injured-player rule. The bleeding must be stopped, the wound covered, the uniform and/or body appropriately cleaned and/or the uniform changed before returning to competition.

3-5-10d If any player's helmet comes completely off during the down, or subsequent dead-ball action related to the down, and it is not due to a foul by the opponent (PlayPic A), that player must leave the game for at least one down unless halftime or an overtime intermission occurs (PlayPic B). In such circumstances, an officials' time-out occurs. Note that if the player whose helmet comes completely off has possession of the ball, the ball is dead immediately.

3-5-10d If a player's helmet comes completely off during the down and it is directly attributable to a foul by an opponent (PlayPic A), the penalty is enforced but the player need not leave the game (PlayPic B).

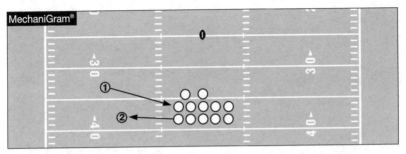

3-7-1 A replaced player must begin to leave the field within three seconds. The three seconds begins when a player becomes a replaced player as defined in 2-32-12 and a substitute becomes a player as defined in 2-32-15. It is not a foul to break a huddle with more than 11 players as long as the replaced player begins to leave the field within three seconds.

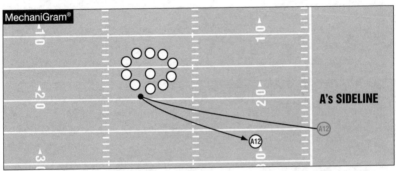

3-7-2 A player, replaced player or a substitute who is unable to complete the substitution is required to leave the field at the side on which his team box is located.

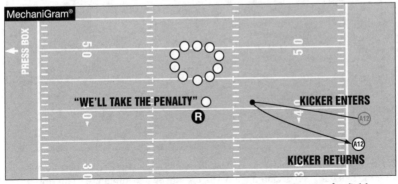

3-7-3 Following a third-down play, a substitute for Team A enters the field for an apparent punting situation. However, a foul has occurred during the down and Team A accepts the penalty. The substitute who previously entered is allowed to return to his team box since the penalty acceptance cancels the unwanted substitution.

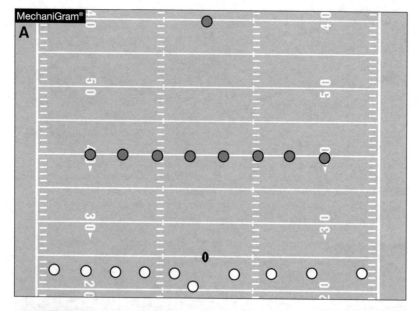

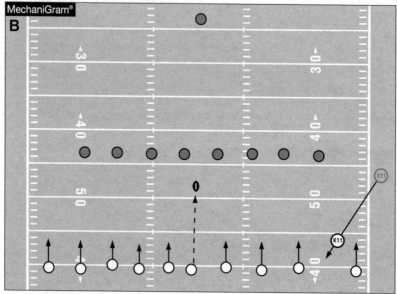

3-7-5 In (A), K has 10 players on the field. Although K11 is in the neutral zone after the ball has been declared ready (B), it is not encroachment. An entering substitute is not a player for encroachment purposes until he reaches his team's side of the neutral zone. Since the ball is kicked with K11 in the neutral zone, the ball is live and it is an illegal-substitution foul for not being on his team's side of the neutral zone when the ball is kicked.

Rule 4

Ball in Play, Dead Ball and Out of Bounds

There are two ways to put the ball in play, with a free kick or with a snap. The ball remains dead and a down is not begun if a snap or free kick is attempted before the ball is ready for play, or there is an illegal snap or other snap infraction. Each half is started with a kickoff. A kickoff also puts the ball in play after a successful field goal and following a try. A free kick follows a safety and if chosen, following a fair catch or awarded catch.

The ball becomes dead and the down is ended:

1. When a runner goes out of bounds or his forward progress is stopped.
2. When a live ball goes out of bounds.
3. When a forward pass (legal or illegal) is incomplete.
4. When a legal kick breaks the plane of R's goal line, unless a field goal is scored.
5. When a loose ball is on the ground and no player attempts to secure possession.
6. When a loose ball is simultaneously caught or recovered by opposing players.
7. When a loose ball is touched by or touches anything inbounds other than a player, substitute, game official, the ground, etc.
8. When the kickers catch or recover any free kick.
9. When the kickers catch or recover a scrimmage kick beyond the neutral zone.
10. When prior to any touching by R, the kickers touch a scrimmage kick beyond the neutral zone after it has come to rest.
11. Following a valid or invalid fair-catch signal when the kick is caught or recovered by R.
12. When a touchdown or field goal is scored.
13. During a try when B secures possession or it is apparent the kick will not score.
14. When the helmet comes completely off a player in possession of the ball.
15. Whenever a game official sounds a whistle inadvertently.

When the ball goes out of bounds, the out-of-bounds spot is fixed by the yard line through the ball's foremost point. When a runner goes out of bounds, the inbounds spot is fixed by the yard line through the foremost point of the ball at the time the runner crosses the plane of the sideline.

4-2-2 EXCEPTION 2 The ball remains live if the holder rises and catches or recovers an errant snap (A) and immediately returns his knee(s) to the ground (B) and places the ball for a kick (C) or again rises to advance, hand, kick or pass (D).

4-2-2a EXCEPTION 2 The snap in (A) is errant. The ball remains live if the holder rises and catches or recovers an errant snap and immediately returns his knee(s) to the ground (B) and places the ball for a kick or again rises to advance, hand, kick or pass (C).

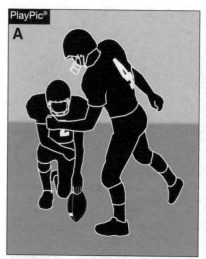

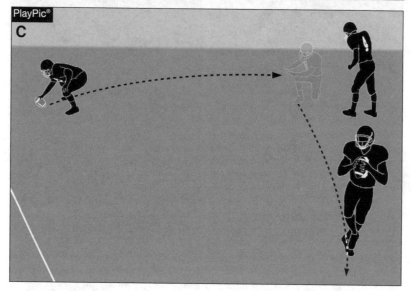

4-2-2a EXCEPTION No. 4 is in position to kick and the holder has a knee(s) on the ground at the snap in (A). The exception to the basic dead-ball rule is in effect when both these conditions are being met at the snap. The ball remains live for a kick as in (B), or if the holder rises with the ball (C) to run, pass or drop kick.

4-2-2a EXCEPTION A holder with his knee(s) on the ground who has a teammate in position to kick at the snap as in (A), is allowed to rise to catch or recover an errant snap. The ball remains live if he goes to his knee(s) immediately after catching or recovering the snap. The holder is then allowed in (C) or (D) to do what he could have done if the snap had been accurate and he had not risen from his knee(s) to begin with. If the snap is muffed or the holder fumbles, he may recover with his knee(s) on the ground and place the ball for a kick or he may rise with it.

BACKWARD
PASS

4-2-2e The backward pass is not caught in (A). When opposing players simultaneously possess a backward pass, as in (B), the ball becomes dead immediately. This ball belongs to the passing team.

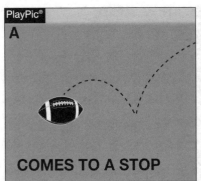

4-2-2f When a scrimmage kick rolls to a complete stop (A) and it is touched by K (B), the covering official will immediately sound his whistle to indicate the ball is dead. In (C) the R player is advancing with a dead ball. Touching by K of a scrimmage kick at rest is not first touching.

4-2-3b The inadvertent-whistle procedure is the same for action in (A), (B) and (C). If the ball is loose and the whistle sounds following an illegal kick, fumble, illegal forward pass or backward pass, the team last in possession may take the results of the play where possession was lost or replay the down. In (A) or (C), if the penalty is accepted, the administration of the foul takes precedence over the inadvertent whistle.

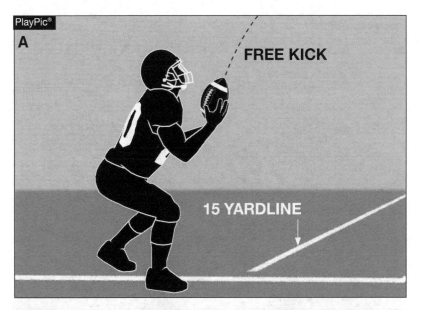

4-3-1 In (A), since the receiver possesses the free kick before he touched out of bounds with the ball inside the sideline plane, he is considered to have caused the ball to be out of bounds. The ball will be put in play at the inbounds spot on the 14-yard line. In (B), since there was no touching by R prior to the player being out of bounds, K has caused the free kick to go out of bounds R may either put the ball in play from the inbounds spot, put the ball in play 25 yards beyond the previous spot, or have the 5-yard penalty enforced against the kicking team from the previous spot and kick off again.

RUNNER HIT BY TACKLER

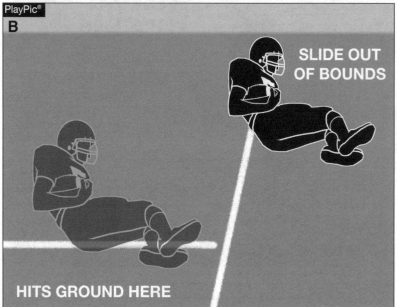

SLIDE OUT OF BOUNDS

HITS GROUND HERE

4-3-2 The runner is inbounds when he is hit by an opponent (A). The ball is dead when the runner hits the ground (B). Even though the runner slides out of bounds, the ball has not been out of bounds and the clock continues to run. The ball is placed at its forward point where the ball became dead. The runner is down when any part of his person, other than hand or foot, touches the ground.

4-3-3 A ball in player possession is out of bounds when the runner or the ball touches anything, other than another player or game official, which is on or outside the sideline or end line. The spot where the ball becomes dead is under the foremost point of the ball in possession of the runner when he crosses the plane of the sideline at B's one-yard line (A). No touchdown is scored in (B) since the runner was airborne and was not touching inbounds when the ball broke the plane of the goal-line extended.

Rule 5

Series of Downs, Number of Downs and Team Possession After Penalty

The team which puts the ball in play by scrimmage after a free kick, touchback or fair catch, is awarded a series of four consecutively numbered downs in which to advance the ball to or beyond the line to gain. A new series is awarded if the ball belongs to the offensive team on or beyond the line to gain. It is also a new series and the ball will belong to the defensive team at the end of any down, if B gained possession during that down, or at the end of a fourth down, if the offensive team was in possession behind the line to gain. If a receiver is the first to touch a scrimmage kick while it is beyond the neutral zone, a new series will be awarded to the team in possession at the end of the down, unless the penalty is accepted for a non post-scrimmage kick foul which occurred before the kick ended.

When a penalty is declined, the number of the next down is the same as if the foul had not occurred. When a foul by A (or K) or B (or R) occurs during a scrimmage down and before any change of team possession, and before a receiver is first to touch a scrimmage kick while it is beyond the neutral zone, the ball belongs to A (or K) after penalty enforcement. The number of the next down is the same as that of the down during which the foul occurred unless acceptance of the penalty carries an automatic first down or loss of down, or the penalty enforcement or advance results in a first down. The loss of down aspect of a penalty has no significance following a change of possession or if the line to gain is reached after enforcement.

When a foul by A or B occurs prior to a scrimmage down, or simultaneously with the snap, the number of the next down after enforcement is the same as the number established before the foul occurred, unless enforcement for a foul by B results in a first down. After a distance penalty, the ball belongs to the team in possession at the time of the foul. Team possession may then change if a new series is awarded.

A. R TOUCHES

B. K HOLDS

C. R RECOVERS

5-1-3d R may choose to decline the penalty and take the results of the play and keep the ball at the spot of recovery. If they accept the penalty for the holding foul, K will replay the down after enforcement from the previous spot. The foul occurred during a loose-ball play.

A. R TOUCHES

B. K HOLDS

C. R RECOVERS

5-1-3f The series is not ended if K accepts the penalty for the foul during a loose-ball play. In this play, K will undoubtedly take the results of the play, decline the penalty and take the ball at the spot of recovery as this is not a PSK foul, so acceptance would result in a replay.

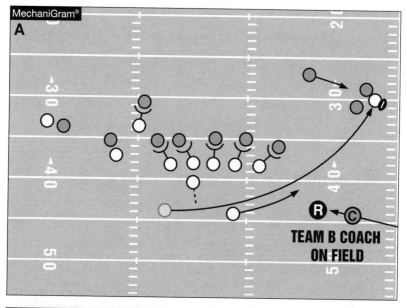

TEAM B COACH
ON FIELD

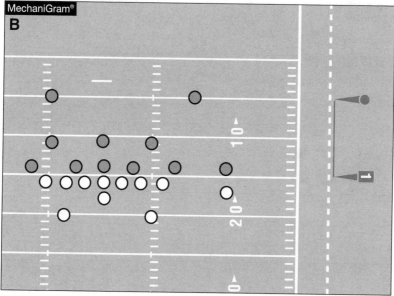

5-3-1 When a new series is gained as in (A), the penalty for the unsportsmanlike foul is administered before the line to gain is established. In (B), the line-to-gain indicator and down marker indicator are then set, making it first and 10 for Team A.

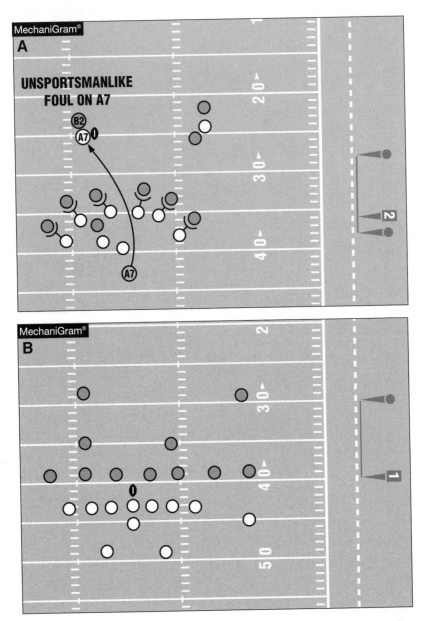

5-3-1 Team A gains a first down, but A7 commits an unsportsmanlike foul after the down in (A) Since the foul occurred prior to the subsequent ready-for-play signal, the line to gain is established following penalty enforcement. It is first and 10 for Team A in (B).

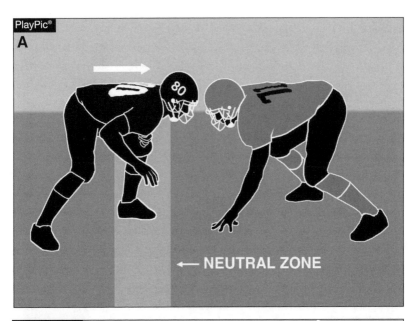

NEUTRAL ZONE

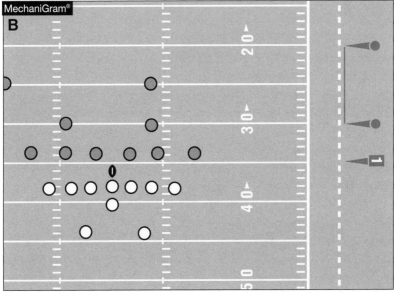

5-3-1 Following the ready-for-play signal on first down, No. 80 encroaches (A). It is first and 15 for Team A following penalty administration (B). A foul after the ready is the only situation where it will be more than first and 10 for Team A to start a new series.

5-3-1 Team A is short of the line to gain on a fourth-down play after enforcement of all live-ball fouls, which dictates it is a new series for Team B. The penalty for the dead-ball illegal personal contact seen in (A) is enforced before the chain and box are set for B's series. It is first and 10 for Team B at B's 35-yard line (B).

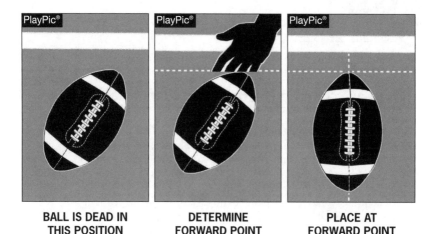

| **BALL IS DEAD IN THIS POSITION** | **DETERMINE FORWARD POINT** | **PLACE AT FORWARD POINT** |

5-3-2 Whenever a measurement is required, the ball shall be placed with its long axis parallel with the sideline before measurement. If it is a first down, the referee gives the signal, spots it and marks it ready for play. If the line to gain has not been reached, the referee signals the distance needed to both sides.

Rule 6

Kicking the Ball and Fair Catch

A free kick is used to put the ball in play to start a free-kick down. A free-kick line is established for each team and is always 10 yards apart. If not moved because of a penalty, K's free-kick line for a kickoff is its 40-yard line, its 20-yard line for a kick following a safety, and the yard line through the spot of the catch following a fair catch.

The offensive team may punt, drop kick or placekick from in or behind the neutral zone before team possession has changed Such a kick is a scrimmage kick. When any member of the kicking team touches a scrimmage kick between the goal lines and beyond the neutral zone, before it is touched by a member of the receiving team and before the ball has come to rest, it is first touching. First touching does not cause the ball to become dead.

Any receiver may signal for a fair catch while any kick is in flight. Any receiver who gives a valid or invalid fair-catch signal is prohibited from blocking until the kick has ended.

If any receiver gives a valid signal for a fair catch and he catches the free kick in or beyond the neutral zone and between the goal lines, or catches the scrimmage kick beyond the neutral zone and between the goal lines, it is a fair catch and the ball becomes dead. Only the receiver who gives a valid signal is afforded protection and only where a fair catch may be made. If, after a receiver gives a valid signal, the catch is made by a teammate, it is not a fair catch but the ball becomes dead. Following a valid or invalid signal by the receiving team, the ball becomes dead when caught or recovered by any receiver.

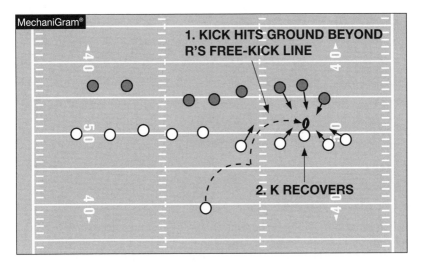

1. KICK HITS GROUND BEYOND R'S FREE-KICK LINE

2. K RECOVERS

6-1-5 If the free kick has gone beyond the plane of the receiver's free-kick line and has touched the ground, any K player may then recover. Both conditions must be met — has touched the ground and has gone beyond the plane. The order of occurrence has no bearing on the fact that K may then recover K may not advance a recovered kick.

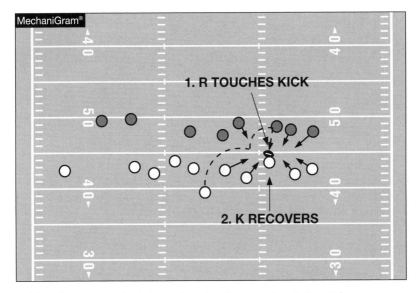

1. R TOUCHES KICK

2. K RECOVERS

6-1-5 When the free kick is touched first by a receiver before it has gone 10 yards, it may be recovered by any K player. The recovery causes the ball to become dead and the down is ended. No K player may advance the recovered kick. However, it is a first down for K.

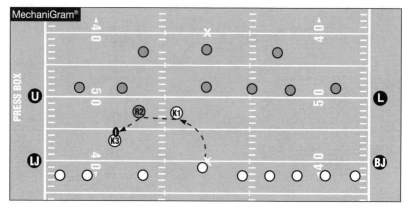

6-1-5 K1's muff in the neutral zone on a free kick causes the ball to touch R2 and K3 recovers. Because R2's touching was caused by K1's muff, the touching by R2 is ignored as they will decline first touching. It will be R's ball at the spot of K3's recovery.

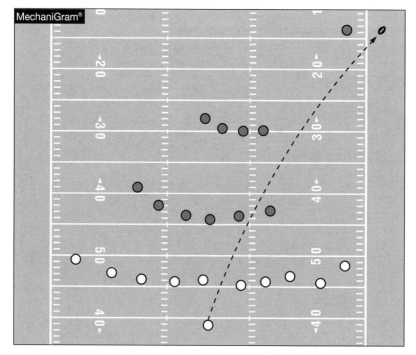

6-1-8 It is a foul if a free kick goes out of bounds between the goal lines, and it was not touched by R. R may decline the penalty and take the ball at the inbounds spot or 25 yards from the previous spot, or accept the 5-yard penalty and have K rekick.

6-1-9 R's No. 80 muffs the kick. There is no recovery by K as No. 5 first contacts the ground out of bounds. R will put the ball in play at the inbounds spot.

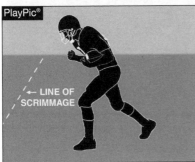

6-2-3 When a field-goal attempt fails, it is treated like any scrimmage kick and the ball remains live until the down ends Since K recovered behind the neutral zone, they may advance. Game officials must be alert and not confuse a field-goal attempt with a try. When it is apparent there will be no score from a kick try, the down is ended.

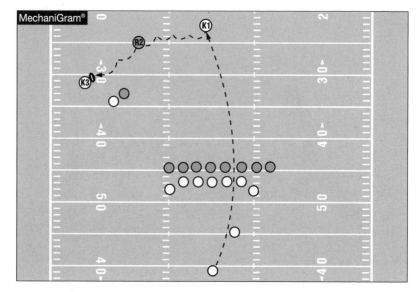

6-2-4 K1 legally bats the scrimmage kick, which deflects off R2. The loose ball is recovered by K3. Because R2's touching was caused by K1's bat, the touching is ignored. R may take the ball at the spot of K3's recovery.

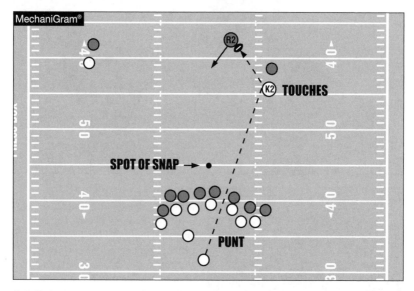

6-2-5 First touching by the kicking team does not cause the ball to become dead. This is a legal advance. The right of R to take the ball at the spot of first touching by K is canceled if R touches the kick and thereafter commits a foul or if the penalty is accepted for any foul committed during the down.

6-2-6 The neutral zone is expanded up to a maximum of 2 yards during a scrimmage down. No. 70 has touched a low scrimmage kick in the expanded neutral zone. The touching of a low scrimmage kick by any player is ignored if the touching is in or behind the expanded neutral zone.

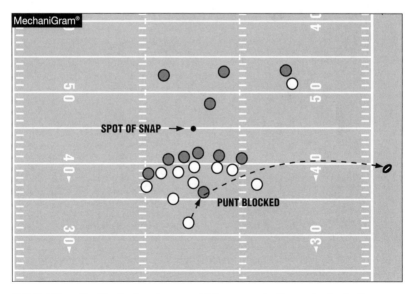

6-2-7 When the blocked scrimmage kick goes out of bounds, the ball belongs to the receiving team at the inbounds spot. This is true regardless of the down and distance when the scrimmage kick was made or where it went out of bounds between the goal line.

END ZONE

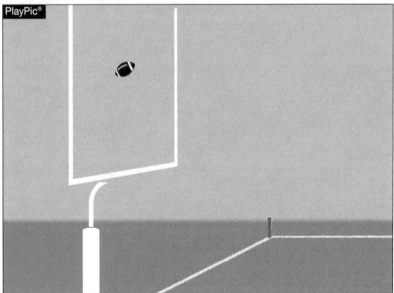

6-3-1 When a potential scoring kick in flight is touched by R in his end zone, it does not become dead if the ball thereafter passes through the goal. The field goal counts. It would also count if the ball touched the crossbar or uprights and deflected through the goal. If R jumps up and blocks the kick away from the goalposts, it causes the ball to become dead immediately; and, on a field goal, it is a touchback.

6-5-1 This is a legal block by R's No. 36 even though R's No. 80 may not advance if the kick is caught or recovered as a valid fair-catch signal was given. However, No. 80 may not block until the kick ends because he has signaled

6-5-6 Kick-catching interference. R has the option of taking the results of the play, accepting an awarded fair catch at the spot of the foul, accepting a 15-yard penalty from the spot of an awarded fair catch, or replaying the down after having the penalty enforced from the previous spot.

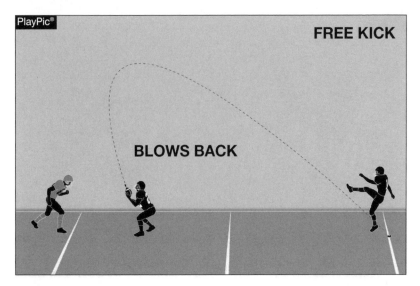

6-5-6 It is kick-catching interference when the kickers touch a free kick in flight. It makes no difference whether or not the ball has been beyond the receiver's free-kick line. This restriction ends after a receiver touches the kick. R may choose an awarded fair catch at the spot of the foul with no distance penalty or have the distance penalty enforced from the previous spot and rekick.

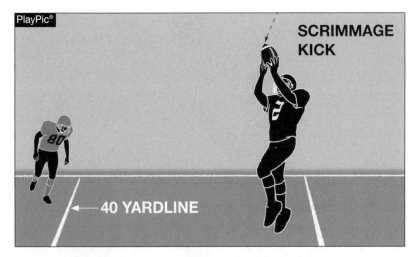

6-5-6 EXCEPTION A member of the kicking team legally catches a scrimmage kick beyond the neutral zone. This is only permissible when no member of the receiving team is in position to catch the ball. There is no requirement that the receiver must make or attempt to make a catch — only that he is in position where he could make a catch if he desired.

6-5-6 EXCEPTION Two R players are in position to attempt a catch. The opponent commits kick-catching interference. The receivers must be given an unmolested opportunity to catch the kick. The ball becomes dead with the catch. R may accept an awarded fair catch at the spot of the foul, accept a 15-yard penalty from the spot of an awarded fair catch, or a replay of the down after having the penalty enforced from the previous spot.

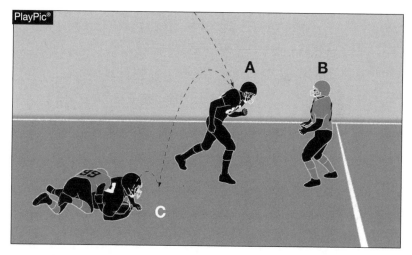

6-5-6 EXCEPTION The punt in flight hits another K player in the shoulder as he goes downfield to cover the kick (A). A receiver is in position to make a catch (B). It is kick-catching interference. R may accept an awarded fair catch at the spot of the foul or accept the penalty of 15 yards from the previous spot and a replay of the down K's recovery (C) is negated.

6-5-6 EXCEPTION This is a legal play. The kickers may touch, bat or muff a grounded free kick even if an R player is in position to make the catch. The receivers may take the results of the play or the ball at the spot of first touching by K.

Rule 7

Snapping, Handing and Passing the Ball

For any scrimmage down, the ball may only become live with a legal snap. A snap is the legal act of passing or handing the ball from its position on the ground in a quick and continuous backward motion of the hand(s) during which the ball immediately leaves the hand(s). A snap ends when the ball touches the ground or a backfield player before it touches a Team A lineman.

The snap begins when the snapper first moves the ball other than in adjustment. The snapper is allowed to make certain preliminary adjustments while not changing the location of the ball. These preliminary movements may be made, but both hands may not be taken off the ball once the snapper has placed a hand(s) on the ball.

After the ball is ready and before the snap, each player of Team A must momentarily be within inside the 9-yard marks before the ball is snapped. Not more than one A player may be in motion at the snap and then only if such motion is not toward B's goal line. After a huddle or shift, all players of A must come to a stop and remain simultaneously stationary for at least one second before the snap.

A forward pass may be thrown only by the team which has put the ball in play from scrimmage, provided the ball is released with both feet of the passer in or behind the neutral zone. There may be only one legal forward pass during a down. During a pass, the ball travels in flight, that is, is thrown rather than handed forward.

During a forward pass, there are at least five ineligible receivers. On a pass which goes beyond the neutral zone, ineligibles may not go beyond the neutral zone before the pass is in flight. Ineligibles may go downfield if the pass does not go beyond the expanded neutral zone. When a forward pass is touched by a defensive player, all A players become eligible immediately.

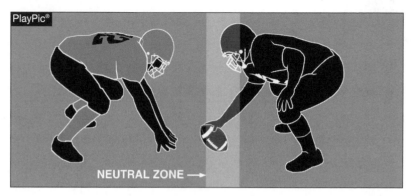
NEUTRAL ZONE →

7-1 A scrimmage down is started with a snap. The snapper's feet must be behind the neutral zone. His head may be in the neutral zone, but not beyond the foremost point of the ball. The ball may be preliminarily adjusted after which the snapper may not make a movement that simulates a snap. The snapper may not remove both hands once he has placed a hand(s) on the ball after the ready-for-play. The snap must be one continuous backward motion in which the ball immediately leaves the hand(s) of the snapper and must touch a Team A non-lineman or the ground before it touches a Team A lineman.

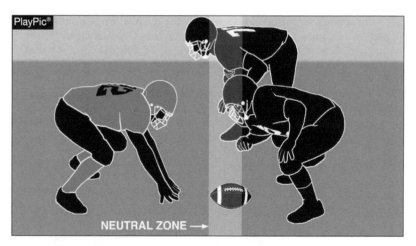
NEUTRAL ZONE →

7-1-6 Encroachment restrictions are not in effect for those in the neutral zone as the snapper has not placed a hand(s) on the ball. The players who are in the neutral zone may move and be out of the neutral zone before the snapper puts his hand(s), on the ball. Before the snapper places his hand(s) on the ball it is encroachment for any other player to touch the ball or an opponent or be in the zone to give defensive signals. All other encroachment restrictions begin after the ready-for-play when the snapper places his hand(s) on the ball.

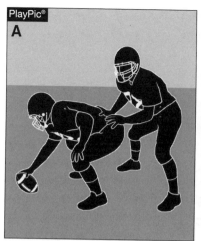

7-1-7a When the quarterback "chucks" his hands under the center (A) or bobs his head (B), it simulates snap action and is a false start. Jerky movements which simulate the beginning of the down or acts clearly intended to cause B to encroach are false starts. These acts must be judged on their own merits rather than whether or not B encroaches.

7-2-3 If the ball is snapped, this would be an illegal formation foul at the snap. Of the A players who are not on their line at the snap, only one player may penetrate through the waistline of his nearest teammate who is on the line, and he must be in position to receive the snap, even though he is not required to receive it.

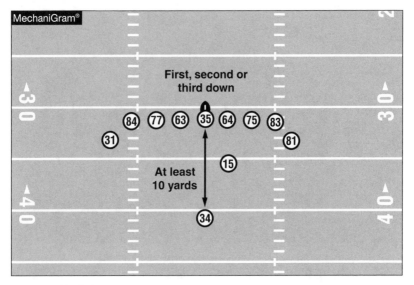

7-2-5 EXCEPTION 1 Illegal numbering. On first, second or third down, if the formation has no player with a knee on the ground in position to receive the long snap and another in position to be a kicker, it is a scrimmage-kick formation but the numbering exception may not be used.

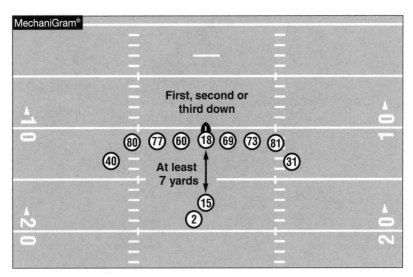

7-2-5 EXCEPTION 1 On first, second or third down, when the kicking team sets or shifts into the scrimmage-kick formation with a holder, only one lineman may wear a number other than 50-79 inclusive. That player must snap the ball and must be positioned between the ends. He remains an ineligible receiver throughout the down unless the opponents touch the ball.

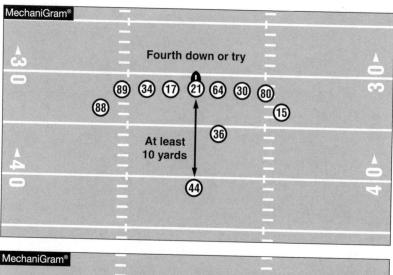

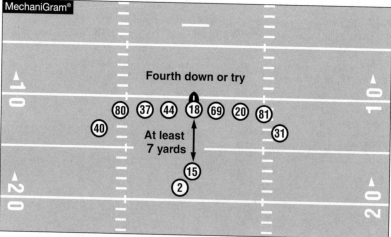

7-2-5 EXCEPTION 2 On fourth down, if the kicking team sets or shifts into either type of legal scrimmage-kick formation, the numbering exception may be used. The formations in A and B are legal.

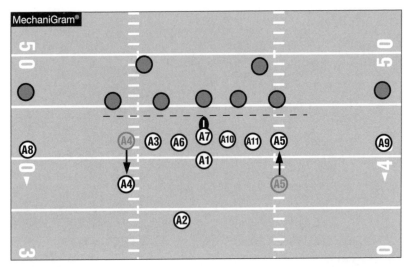

7-2-6 The movement of one or more offensive players to new set positions is a shift. This formation is legal A3 is now on the end of the line; if he is also wearing an eligible receiver's number, he is an eligible receiver. A9 is also on the end of the line and is eligible if he is wearing an eligible receiver's number. Following a shift, all 11 players must simultaneously meet the one-second motionless requirement prior to the snap.

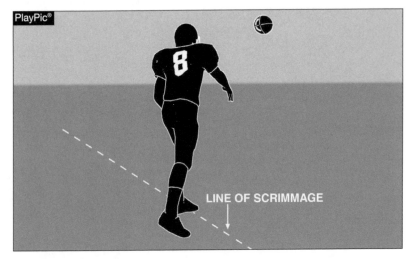

7-5-2b The passer has one foot beyond the plane of the neutral zone when he releases the ball on a forward pass. The pass is illegal. An illegal forward pass is part of a running play with the end of the run being the spot from which the pass is thrown.

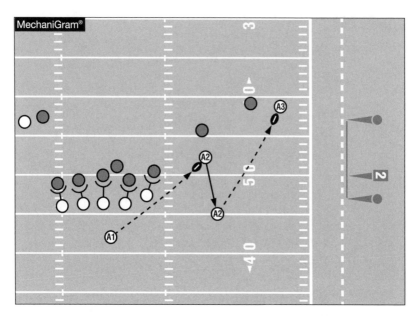

7-5-2c A1 throws a pass to A2 who is beyond the line of scrimmage A2 retreats behind the line of scrimmage and then throws a pass to A3. The pass by A2 is an illegal pass as only one forward pass be thrown.

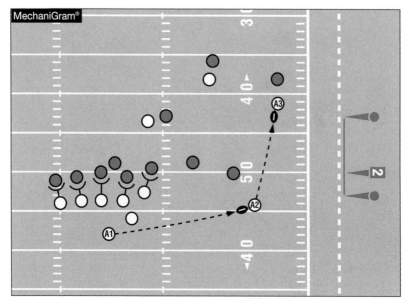

7-5-2c A1 throws a forward pass to A2 who throws second to A3. The pass by A2 is an illegal pass.

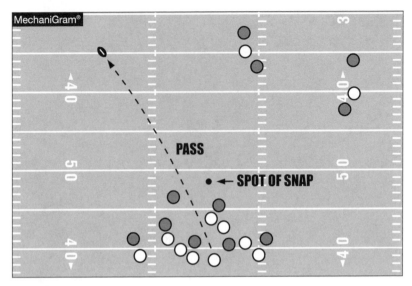

7-5-2d This is an illegal forward pass as it was intentionally thrown into an area not occupied by an eligible offensive receiver. If the referee judges it was also done to conserve time, he shall start the clock on the ready. If accepted, the penalty is enforced from the end of the run — the spot of the pass.

7-5-2e EXCEPTION The illustration shows how the quarterback stops the clock legally. Following the hand-to-hand snap, the ball is immediately thrown forward to the ground as he steps backward to clear himself from the line play.

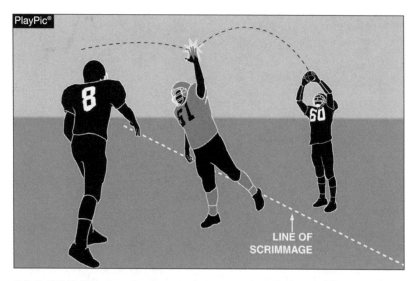

7-5-7, 7-5-9 Pass interference restrictions apply only beyond the neutral zone and only if the legal forward pass, untouched by the defense in or behind the neutral zone, crosses the neutral zone. The touching by No. 61 makes No. 60 an eligible receiver.

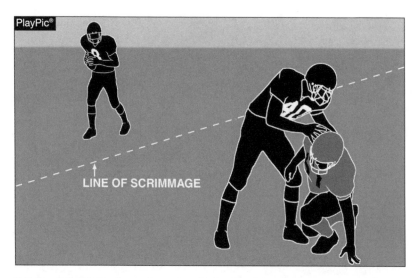

7-5-8a, 7-5-10 During a down in which a legal forward pass crossed the neutral zone, a Team A receiver may not contact an opponent with his hands beyond the neutral zone for any purpose until the pass has touched a player. If a forward pass is thrown beyond the neutral zone, the contact results in offensive pass interference. Team A restrictions begin with the snap.

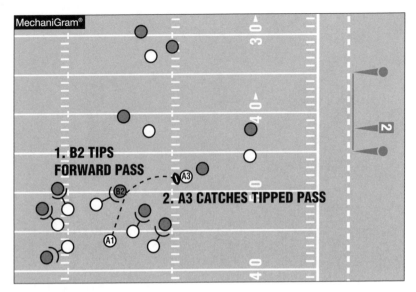

7-5-9, 7-5-10 Tipped pass by B2. Lineman A3 is eligible as the pass was tipped by B behind the line of scrimmage Pass restrictions for both A and B ended when B touched the pass.

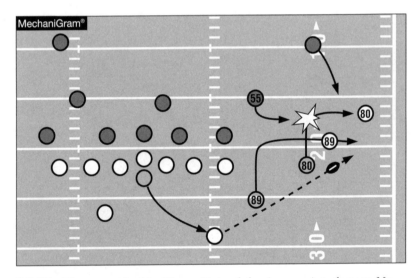

7-5-10a The contact by No. 55 constitutes defensive pass interference. No. 80 is entitled to his position and is entitled to maintain that position on the field. Defensive pass interference carries a 15-yard penalty and a replay of the down. Once No. 80 occupies the same yard line as No. 55, he is no longer a potential blocker.

7-5-10b Defensive pass interference. No. 28 has directed his attention to blocking the vision of the receiver which indicates an intent to hinder the receiver rather than catch or bat the ball and it is, therefore, interference even if there is no contact.

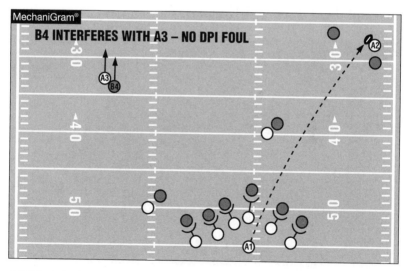

7-5-11 A foul or contact away from the direction of the pass is not pass interference. However, this does not take away the restrictions on illegal use of hands, holding, or a personal foul.

7-5-11a When two opposing eligible pass receivers are making a simultaneous and bona fide attempt to catch or bat the ball, and there is unavoidable contact, it is not a foul. The defender and receiver both have a right to attempt to gain possession of the pass.

7-5-12 An ineligible receiver may block an opponent who is within 1 yard of his line of scrimmage at the snap and drive him back up to 2 yards into the defensive secondary. The neutral zone is expanded to this extent during a forward pass which crosses the neutral zone. If the defensive player is not on his line of scrimmage at the snap, it is pass interference to contact him downfield.

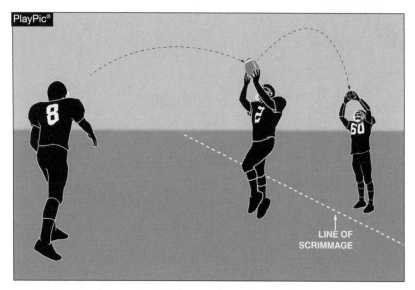

7-5-12 Ineligible receiver downfield and illegal touching by No. 60 because he was beyond the neutral zone before the legal forward pass which crossed the neutral zone was thrown. On a pass that crosses the neutral zone, touching by A does not make the ineligible receivers eligible.

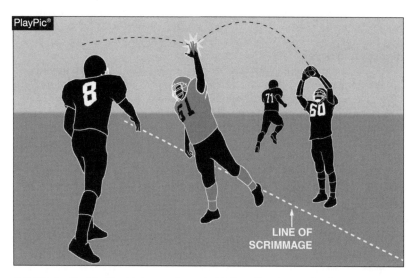

7-5-12 Ineligible No. 71 is not downfield illegally, due to the fact No. 61 touched the ball prior to the legal forward pass crossing the neutral zone.

Rule 8

Scoring Plays and Touchback

Anytime a live ball, in the possession of a runner, penetrates the plane of the opponent's goal line or touches the goal line, it is a touchdown. It is also a touchdown when a player gains possession of a live ball in his opponent's end zone.

Following a touchdown, the scoring team is entitled to a try from the opponent's 3-yard line. During the try, a successful field goal will score one point and two points will be scored if a scrimmage play results in what would be a touchdown under rules governing play at other times in the game. One point will be scored if the play results in what would normally be a safety in B's end zone. The try is waived if the touchdown is scored during the last down of the fourth period and the outcome of the game has been decided and the point(s) is not required for playoff qualification.

A safety is scored when a player gives the ball the force or impetus that carries it across his own goal line, and it becomes dead there not in possession of its opponents. It is also a safety when a player on offense commits any foul for which the penalty is accepted and measurement is from a spot in his end zone.

A field goal is scored when a player drop kicks or placekicks the ball from scrimmage or from a free kick after a fair catch or awarded catch, so that the ball passes above the crossbar and between the vertical uprights of his opponent's goal.

It is a touchback when any kick (except a successful field-goal attempt) breaks the plane of R's goal line or if a forward pass which is intercepted in B's end zone becomes dead there in B's possession. A fumble, muff or bat of a backward pass or fumble, results in a touchback when the force or the new force which sends the ball to or across the opponent's goal line is provided by the offensive team and the defense is in team possession, or the ball is out of bounds when it becomes dead on or behind the goal line. If any kick becomes dead on or behind the kicker's goal line with the ball in possession of the kicking team and the new force was a muff or a bat of the kick by the receiver after it touched the ground, it is a touchback.

8-2-1 It is a touchdown whenever the live ball, in possession of a runner, breaks the vertical plane of the opponent's goal line, regardless of whether or not the runner is in contact with the ground. The position of the runner's body is of no consequence as long as the ball in his possession breaks the vertical plane of the goal line before he was out of bounds.

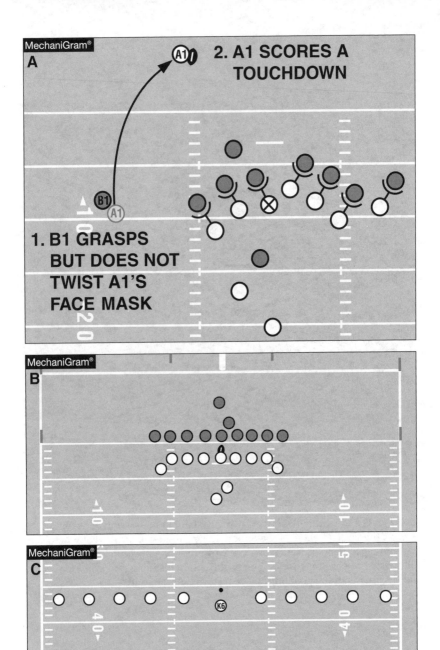

8-2-2 A team that is fouled (other than unsportsmanlike conduct or a nonplayer foul) during a play that results in a touchdown (A) may choose to have the penalty for a live-ball foul enforced on the try (B) or the subsequent kickoff (C).

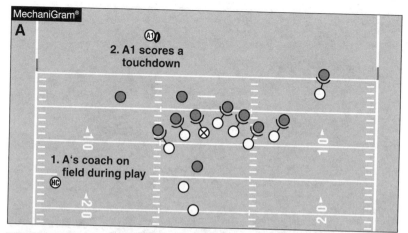

A

2. A1 scores a touchdown

1. A's coach on field during play

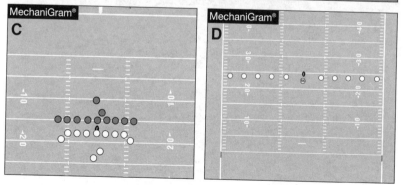

8-2-2, 8-2-3, 8-2-4 During a down that results in a touchdown (MechaniGram A), if either team commits an unsportsmanlike (B) or nonplayer foul the offended team has the choice of enforcement on the try (MechaniGram C) or the subsequent kickoff (MechaniGram D).

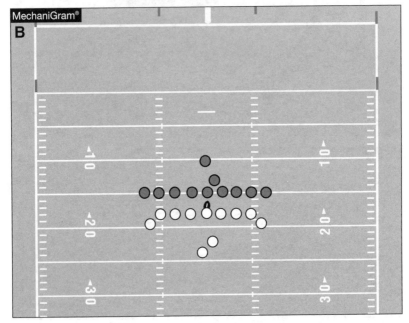

8-2-2, 8-2-3, 8-2-4 The penalty for an unsportsmanlike or nonplayer foul (A) during a down that results in a touchdown on the last timed down of regulation must be enforced on the try (MechaniGram B), as is there is no subsequent kickoff.

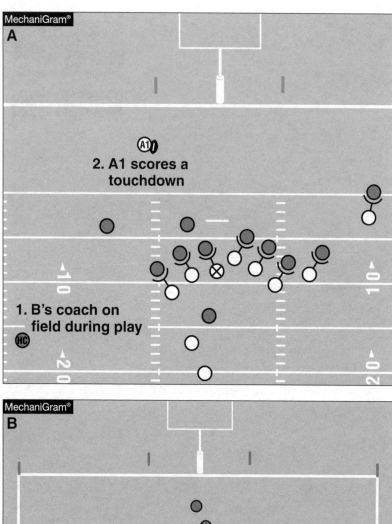

MechaniGram®

A

2. A1 scores a
touchdown

1. B's coach on
field during play

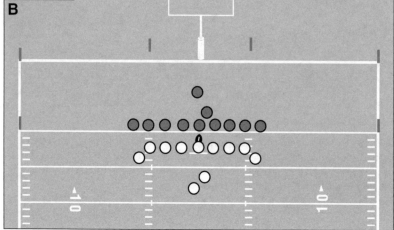

MechaniGram®

B

8-2-2, 8-2-3, 8-2-4, 10-5-1f If during a touchdown-scoring play on the last timed down of the fourth period either team commits a foul that has succeeding-spot enforcement (A), it is not possible to carry over the penalty to an overtime period. The penalty must be enforced on the try (B).

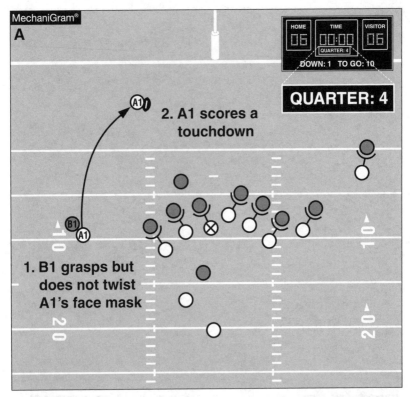

A

2. A1 scores a touchdown

QUARTER: 4

1. B1 grasps but does not twist A1's face mask

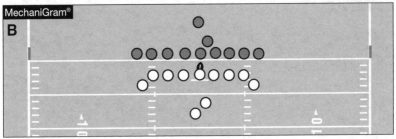

B

8-2-2a The opponent of the scoring team commits a live-ball foul (other than unsportsmanlike conduct or a nonplayer foul) during the last timed down of the fourth quarter and there was no change of possession (A). By rule, the penalty must be enforced on the try (B).

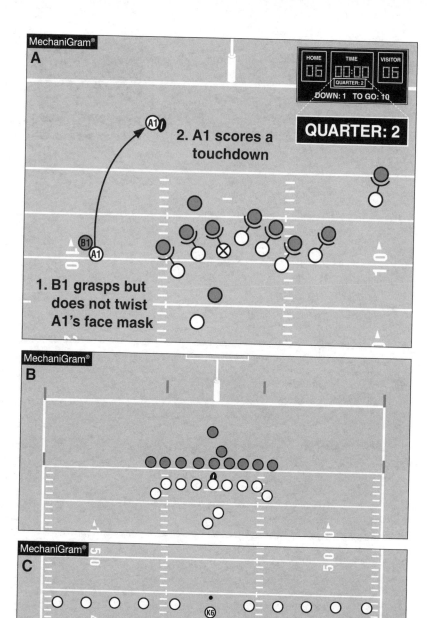

8-2-2a, b The opponent of the scoring team commits a live-ball foul (other than unsportsmanlike conduct or a nonplayer foul) during the last timed down of the second quarter and there was no change of possession (A). The penalty may be enforced on the try (B) or on the subsequent kickoff to start the second half (C).

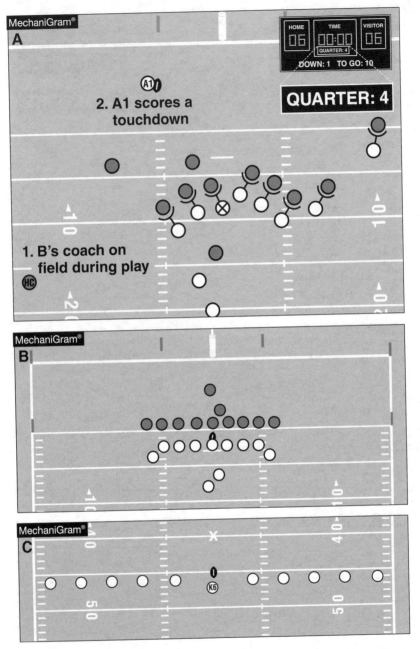

8-2-2a,b; 8-2-3a,b; 8-2-4a,b; 10-5-1f If during a touchdown-scoring play either team commits a foul that has succeeding-spot enforcement (A), the penalty may be enforced on either the try (B) or on the subsequent kickoff (C).

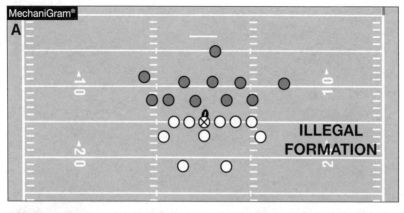

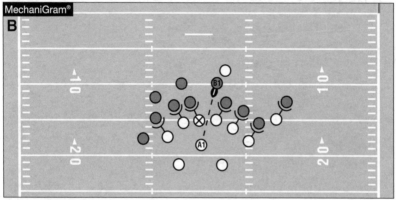

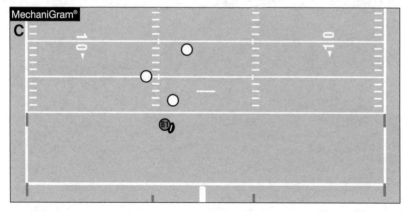

8-2-3, 10-5-3 If the foul is by A before B gains possession and then scores, B has no penalty options, as it must decline A's foul to keep the score (10-5-3). In (A), A is flagged for an illegal formation A1's pass intercepted (B) and returned for a touchdown (C). If B wants to keep the score, it must decline the penalty. There is no option for enforcement on the subsequent kickoff.

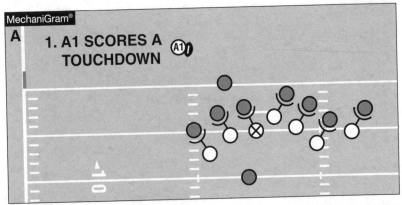

A

1. A1 SCORES A TOUCHDOWN

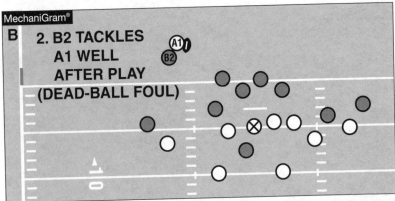

B

2. B2 TACKLES A1 WELL AFTER PLAY (DEAD-BALL FOUL)

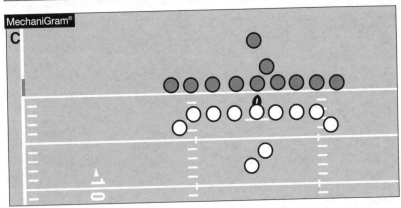

C

8-2-5 The optional penalty enforcement applies on dead-ball fouls that occur prior to the initial ready-for-play on the try. In (A), A1 scores a touchdown Several seconds after the play is over, B2 contacts A1 (B). A has the option to have the penalty enforced from the succeeding spot or on the the subsequent kickoff. Enforcement on the try would result in half-the-distance enforcement (C).

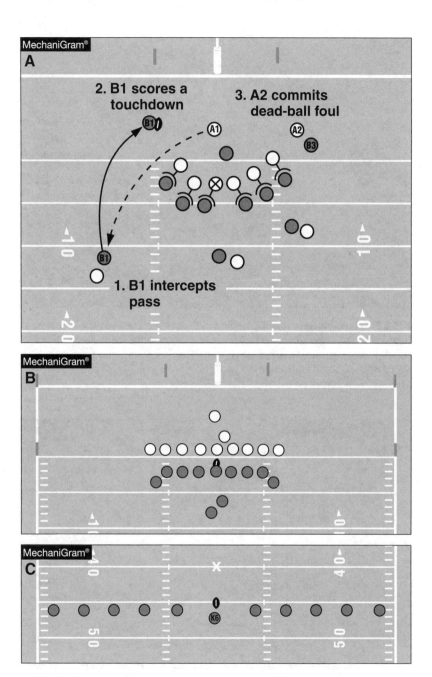

8-2-5, 10-5-1f If either team commits a foul that has succeeding-spot enforcement before the initial ready-for-play signal on the ensuing try following a touchdown-scoring play (A), the penalty may be enforced on either the try (B) or on the subsequent kickoff (C).

8-3-2b When it is apparent a kick will not score during a try, the ball becomes dead immediately. The kick cannot score after the kicked ball touches the ground. There's no way A or B can score any points once the kick fails. Game officials must be aware that after a blocked field-goal attempt, which is not a try, the ball remains live.

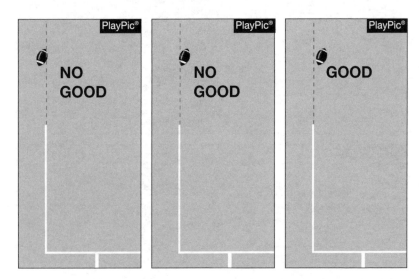

8-4-1 During a field-goal attempt, the kick must pass above the crossbar and between the vertical uprights or the inside edges of the uprights extended in order to be successful. If any part of the ball penetrates the plane of the inside edges of the vertical-uprights extended, it is unsuccessful.

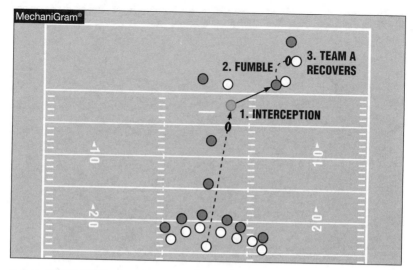

8-5-2a EXCEPTION The Team B player intercepts (1). His original momentum carries him into his own end zone after a catch inside his 5-yard line. If the fumble is recovered by Team A in Team B's end zone (3), it is a touchdown for Team A.

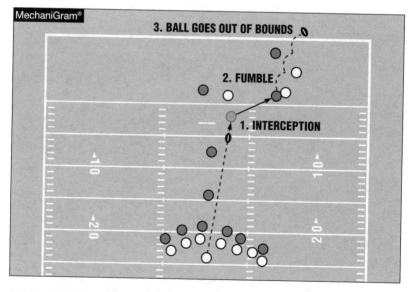

8-5-2a EXCEPTION The Team B player intercepts (1). His original momentum carries him into his own end zone after a catch inside his 5-yard line. If the fumble goes out of bounds behind the goal line (3), it belongs to Team B on the yard line on which it was intercepted.

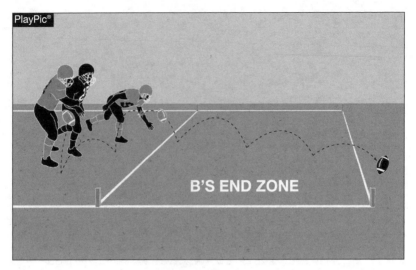

8-5-2b After a fumble has been grounded, a new force may result from a muff or bat. If the covering official rules B's attempted recovery provided a new force causing the ball to go into and through his own end zone, the result is a safety. If B had not added a new force, A's fumble through B's end zone would have been a touchback.

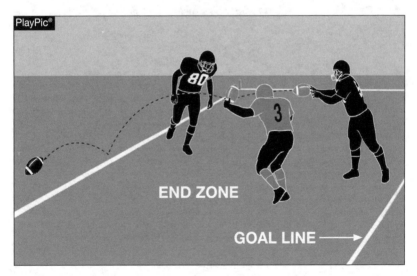

8-5-2b The result of this play is a safety. The force which puts the ball through the end zone is the backward pass No. 3 did not supply a new force as the backward pass had not been grounded when he contacted it.

K'S END ZONE

8-5-2b One receiver blocks the punt and the ball is rolling near the goal line when a teammate touches the ball in an attempt to recover. The covering official must judge whether the ball could have gone into the end zone without the touch Since no new force was given, the original force was supplied by the kick and it is a safety if the ball goes out of bounds from the end zone.

END ZONE

8-5-2c After muffing the snap, No. 11 holds No. 58 to prevent him from recovering the ball. This is a foul by No. 11, for which the penalty is administered toward the end line according to the "all-but-one" principle. The result is a safety. If No. 58 had recovered in the end zone, A's foul could have been declined resulting in a touchdown.

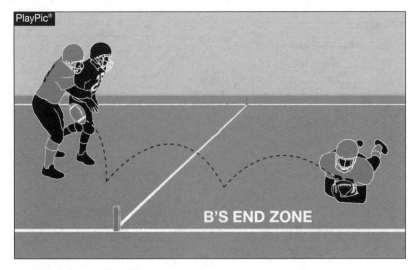

8-5-3c It is a touchback when a fumble is the force which sends the ball from the field of play across the opponent's goal line and the opponent is in possession in the end zone when the ball becomes dead. If the ball is fumbled through the end zone and out of bounds, it also results in a touchback. If A had recovered in the end zone, it would have been a touchdown.

8-5-3d A forward pass is the force which causes the ball to cross the opponent's goal line. Following the interception by B, if the ball becomes dead in Team B's possession in the end zone, the result is a touchback B may run the ball out of the end zone or may down it in the end zone. If B fumbles and A recovers in the end zone, it is a touchdown for A.

Rule 9

Conduct of Players and Others

It must be recognized that participation in sports requires an acceptance of risk of injury. Football is a vigorous, physical contact game and, for this reason, much attention is given to minimizing the risk of injury to the players. In addition to requiring player equipment which offers protection, those responsible for administering the program must be certain coaches teach techniques which are within the rules. Game officials must accept the responsibility for properly administering the rules as written.

In a game in which forceful, physical contact is not only permitted but encouraged, there will invariably be some injury. However, when injury results from techniques taught for the purpose of physically abusing opponents, such techniques must be eliminated.

Blocking by a player either on offense or defense is legal provided it is not: kick-catching interference; forward-pass interference; a personal foul or prohibited contact such as a chop block, etc. Except to bring down the runner, blocking below the waist is legal only if the player(s) is/are on the line of scrimmage and in the zone at the snap, and the block is in the free-blocking zone. A receiver who gives a valid or invalid signal for a fair catch may not block until the kick has ended.

In order to ensure balance between the offense and defense, definite restrictions are placed upon each. An offensive player is restricted in the use of his hands and arms other than in a legal block. A defensive player may use his hands to push or pull an opponent in order to get at a runner or to ward off a blocker or to reach a loose ball which he may retain following possession. It is always a foul for a player on either team to lock his hands while contacting an opponent with his hands or to strike an opponent with the hand, forearm or elbow.

9-2-3c This contact by No. 61 is not a foul since No. 8 is pretending to be a runner. However, the defensive player must exercise reasonable caution in avoiding any unnecessary tackle. A runner or player pretending to be a runner may be contacted from the front or back.

9-2-3d When No. 80 is no longer a potential blocker, contacting the receiver is illegal use of the hands by the defense. Once No. 80 is on the same yard line as the defender, or after he has made his cut away from the defender, he is no longer a potential blocker. If this contact occurs after a forward pass which crosses the neutral zone is in flight, it is defensive pass interference, unless the pass is not in the vicinity of the contact.

9-3-2 The block is legal, even though contact is below the waist. The restriction on blocking below the waist does not apply unless the opponent had one or both feet on the ground. No. 75 has caused the contact to be below the waist when he jumped in an attempt to block the kick.

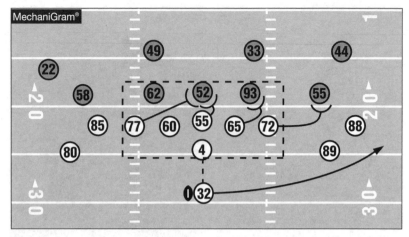

9-3-5a It is legal for offensive linemen to block from behind in the free-blocking zone, provided both players were on their lines of scrimmage and within the zone at the time of the snap and the ball has not left the zone. If the players are on the line of scrimmage but only partially in the zone at the snap, they are considered to be in the zone for purposes of administration. No. 77 could block No. 52 below the waist and No. 65 could block No. 93 below the waist provided the free-blocking zone continued to exist. No. 72 could not block No. 55 below the waist at any time during this play.

9-3-5b The offensive blocker is between the runner and the potential tackler. The defender pushes the blocker from behind above the waist, then continues to pursue and make the tackle. The contact by the defender on the blocker is legal. It is also legal to use hands on the back of an opponent when the ball is loose and the player may legally recover it.

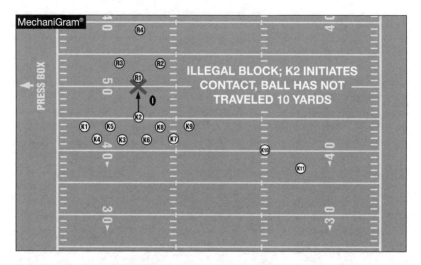

9-3-8 No member of the kicking team shall initiate contact to (block) an opponent on a free kick until the legal kick has traveled 10 yards; the kicking team is eligible to recover a free kicked ball; or the receiving team initiates a block within the neutral zone.

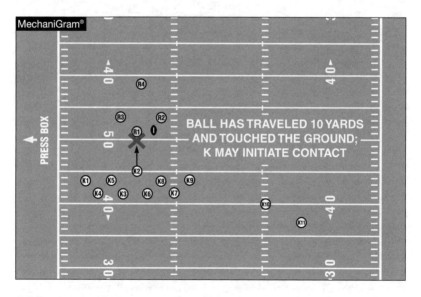

9-3-8 No member of the kicking team shall initiate contact to (block) an opponent on a free kick until the legal kick has traveled 10 yards; the kicking team is eligible to recover a free kicked ball; or the receiving team initiates a block within the neutral zone.

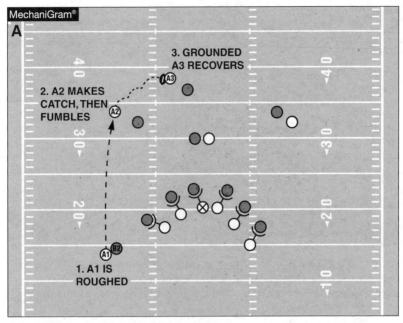

A

3. GROUNDED
A3 RECOVERS

2. A2 MAKES
CATCH, THEN
FUMBLES

1. A1 IS
ROUGHED

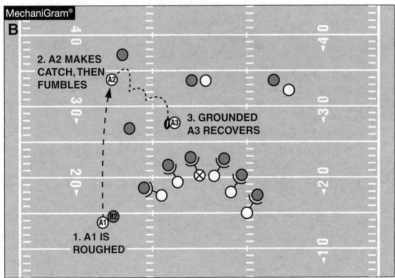

B

2. A2 MAKES
CATCH, THEN
FUMBLES

3. GROUNDED
A3 RECOVERS

1. A1 IS
ROUGHED

9-4 PENALTY For the purpose of roughing the passer, the last spot where A possesses the ball (by run or recovery) is the spot from which to enforce the roughing. In MechaniGram A, A1 is roughed as A2 catches a pass at A's 35-yard line, where he fumbles. Grounded A3 recovers at A's 39-yard line. Enforcement is from A's 39-yard line, which is where the ball was recovered by A. In MechaniGram B, A2's fumble is recovered by grounded A3 at A's 28-yard line. The penalty enforced from the spot of recovery.

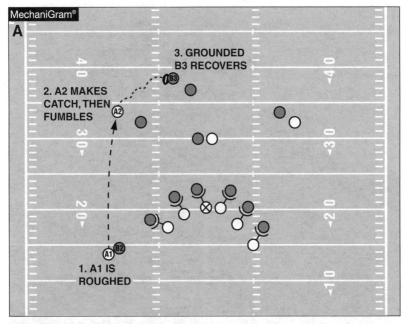

MechaniGram®

A

2. A2 MAKES CATCH, THEN FUMBLES

3. GROUNDED B3 RECOVERS

1. A1 IS ROUGHED

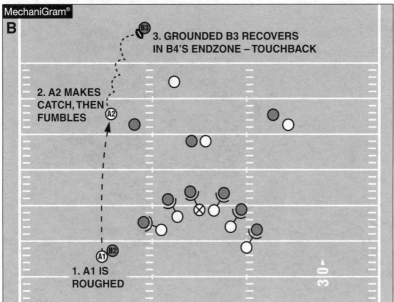

MechaniGram®

B

3. GROUNDED B3 RECOVERS IN B4'S ENDZONE – TOUCHBACK

2. A2 MAKES CATCH, THEN FUMBLES

1. A1 IS ROUGHED

9-4 PENALTY When the passer is roughed and there is a change of team possession or the run ends behind the previous spot, the penalty is enforced from the previous spot. In MechaniGram A, because B recovers the fumble, enforcement is from the previous spot. In MechaniGram B, when the result of the play is a touchback, enforcement is from the previous spot.

9-4-3b The rules provide that it is illegal to contact a player who is clearly out of the play or to make any other contact which is deemed unnecessary and which incites roughness. Also, unwarranted and unnecessary "punishing" of a ball carrier must be eliminated.

9-4-3h PENALTY Grasping the face mask, helmet opening, chin strap or tooth and mouth protector attached to the face mask is a foul. If there is twisting, turning or pulling of the face mask (A), helmet opening, chin strap or tooth and mouth protector attached to a face mask, it is a 15-yard penalty; otherwise it is a 5-yard penalty (B). When in doubt, it is a 15-yard penalty.

9-4-3h Grasping an opponent's tooth and mouth protector attached to the face mask is a foul.

9-4-3i Butt blocking (A and B) and face tackling (C) are both tactics which involve initiating contact with the helmet directly into an opponent in blocking or tackling respectively Both result in a foul for illegal helmet contact.

9-4-3j Striking blows are always illegal. This example of a "clotheslining" tactic by a defensive back must be penalized. The penalty of 15 yards will be measured from the end of the run and the offender shall be disqualified. Tactics such as this have no place in the game.

9-4-3k A horse-collar is a foul. A horse-collar occurs when a defender grabs the runner by the inside back collar of the shoulder pads or jersey, or the inside collar of the side of the shoulder pads or jersey, and subsequently pulls (backward or sideward) that opponent to the ground, even if possession is lost. The penalty is 15 yards and is enforced as a live-ball foul.

9-4-3k If one would-be tackler has grabbed the shoulder pads or collar of the runner, but that opponent is brought down as the result of a more conventional tackle by another player, there is no foul.

9-4-3k No player or nonplayer shall grab the inside back or side collar of the shoulder pads or jersey of the runner and subsequently pull (backward or sideward) that opponent to the ground (horse-collar). The horse-collar foul is enforced as a live-ball foul. Note that it is a horse-collar even if the runner loses possession as a result of the foul.

9-4-3k If the horse-collar tackle (A) is not completed until after the runner crosses B's goal line or a sideline (B), it is enforced as a live-ball foul. Team A may choose enforcement of the 15-yard penalty on the try or on the subsequent kickoff.

FOURTH DOWN

FOURTH DOWN

9-4-3k The horse-collar is to be enforced as a live-ball foul. In PlayPic A, the horse-collar was initiated inbounds but ends out of bounds short of the line-to-gain (PlayPic B). That is a live-ball foul carrying a 15-yard penalty. Enforcement on the play illustrated will result in a first down for A.

9-4-5 In (A), the R player makes only slight contact with the kicker, which only causes the kicker to spin around (B). The covering official could judge no foul on this play.

9-4-5 In (A), the R player makes contact with the kicker, which causes the kicker to be displaced (B). This is intended to illustrate running into the kicker.

9-4-5 In (A), the R player contacts the kicker's plant leg, making the kicker extremely vulnerable. The contact knocks the kicker to the ground (B). This is an example of roughing the kicker.

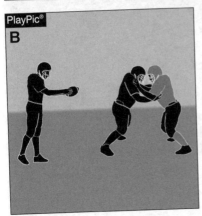

9-4-5 In (A), the kicker takes the snap (A). Another K player blocks an onrushing R player (B). The block causes the R player to contact the kicker (C), knocking him to the ground (D). Because the R player's block caused the contact on the kicker, there is no foul.

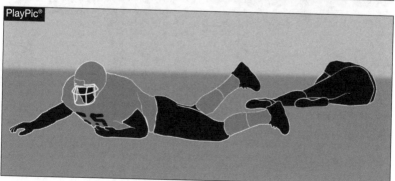

9-4-5 A 15-yard penalty is applicable when there is illegal contact on the kicker/holder. The penalty also carries an automatic first down. A bad snap does not automatically eliminate the kicker's protection from roughing.

9-4-7 No defensive player may use the hand(s) to slap a blocker's head (A). In (B), if the slap is to the head while the ball is in the air to pass, it would be defensive pass interference.

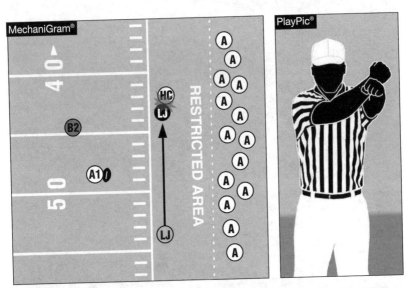

9-4-8 PENALTY If a game official and a nonplayer unintentionally collide in the restricted area while the ball is live, the offended team is penalized 15 yards for illegal personal contact. A second offense would result in ejection of the head coach and a 15-yard penalty from the succeeding spot.

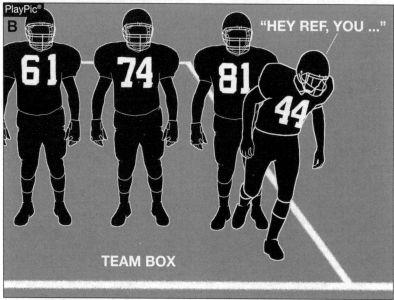

9-5; 9-8 PENALTY No. 44 receives one unsportsmanlike foul for spiking the ball as a player in (A) and a second for foul language as a nonplayer in (B) No. 44 is disqualified upon receiving the second unsportsmanlike foul which carries a 15-yard penalty. Game officials must keep accurate records of unsportsmanlike fouls.

9-5-1c Players must be penalized for prolonged or excessive acts designed to focus attention on themselves Such displays must be penalized without hesitation. The unsportsmanlike act is penalized from the succeeding spot.

9-6-1 Team A receiver No. 80 steps on the sideline and then returns inbounds and catches a forward pass. No. 80 has committed an illegal-participation foul. The spot of the foul is the spot where he returned inbounds. No foul if he does not return inbounds Similar restrictions apply to Team K players.

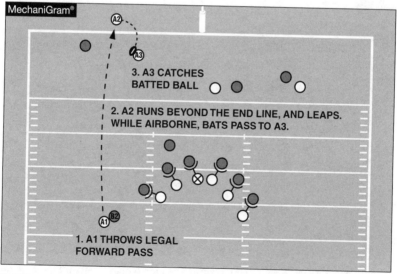

3. A3 CATCHES BATTED BALL

2. A2 RUNS BEYOND THE END LINE, AND LEAPS. WHILE AIRBORNE, BATS PASS TO A3.

1. A1 THROWS LEGAL FORWARD PASS

9-6-2 It is illegal participation if a player intentionally goes out of bounds during the down and returns to the field, intentionally touches the ball, influences the play, or otherwise participates. The penalty is 15 yards from the previous spot.

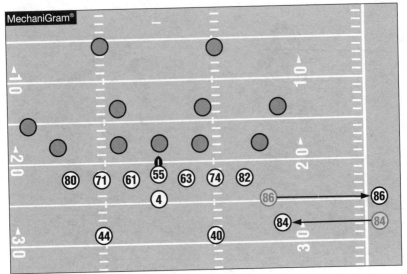

9-6-4c, d It is illegal participation to use a substitution situation to deceive the opponents at or immediately before a snap or free kick. This act becomes a foul at the snap. If the penalty is accepted, it will be enforced from the previous spot.

9-7-2 EXCEPTION K may bat a scrimmage kick which is beyond the neutral zone toward his own goal line. This is legal action. If the bat occurred beyond the plane of the goal line, the ball was already dead, causing it to be a touchback K may also bat a scrimmage kick in flight beyond the neutral zone toward his own goal line if no R player is in position to catch the ball.

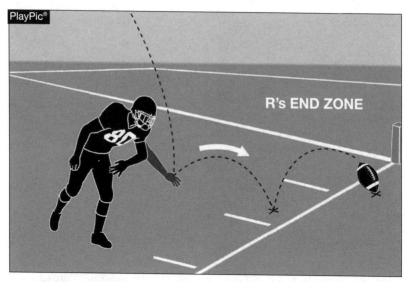

9-7-2 EXCEPTION When the ball is beyond the neutral zone and no Team R player is in position to catch the ball, Team K players may only bat the kick backward (toward their own goal line). Batting the ball forward is a foul.

9-8-1 A second unsportsmanlike foul with a 15-yard penalty by the same member of the coaching staff will cause the coach to be disqualified and removed from the stadium area. He may not communicate with coaches or players from the area or from the press box, he may not be in the team locker room during halftime and must adhere to state association rules upon disqualification.

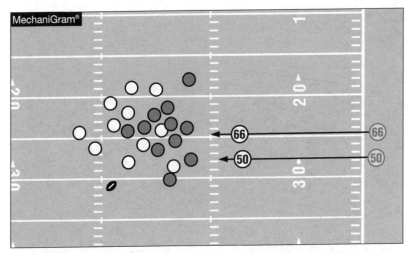

9-8-1l While a fight is taking place on the field, two substitutes of. Team A leave their team box and then enter the field. The two substitutes are each charged with an unsportsmanlike conduct foul and are also disqualified. Two 15-yard penalties will be assessed Substitutes shall not leave the team box during a fight. In addition, the players who are fighting shall be penalized and disqualified.

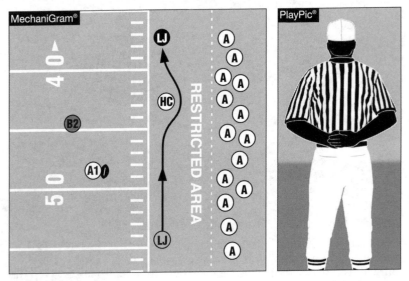

9-8-3 If a player, coach or nonplayer is in the restricted zone while the ball is live but does not contact a game official, a warning is issued for the first offense. The second instance results in a five-yard penalty and each subsequent offense results in a 15-yard unsportsmanlike conduct penalty.

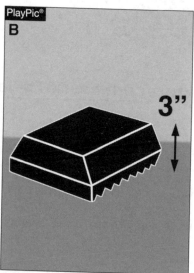

9-9-3, 9-9-4, PENALTY 9-9 Use of kicking tees that elevate the lowest point of the ball more than two inches (A and B) results in a 15-yard penalty enforced under the all-but-one principle. Hiding the ball under a jersey (C) is also an unfair act. The penalty is 15 yards enforced under the all-but-one principle.

Rule 10

Enforcement of Penalties

In the NFHS football rules, the penalty-enforcement philosophy is based upon the principle thata team is entitled to the advantage of distance gained without the assistance of a foul. Because of the all-but-one penalty-enforcement principle, it is not necessary to memorize a long list of different rules. It defines a simplified penalty system. If a foul occurs during a down, the basic spot is determined by the type of play. There are two types of plays:

1. A loose-ball play is action during:
   b. free kick or scrimmage kick.
   c. a legal forward pass.
   d. a backward pass (including the snap), illegal kick or a fumble made by A from in or behind the neutral zone prior to a change of team possession. A loose-ball play also includes the run (or runs) which precedes such legal or illegal kick, legal forward pass, backward pass or fumble.
5. A running play is any action not included in item 1.

If a foul occurs during a loose-ball play, the basic spot is the previous spot with the exception of post-scrimmage kick fouls. For a running play, it is the spot where the related run ends.

While it is possible to have several running plays during a down, with each one having its own basic spot — where the related run ended — there can be only one loose-ball play, during a down.

If a live-ball foul is followed by a dead-ball foul, the penalty for the live-ball foul will be administered in accordance with the all-but-one principle. The dead-ball foul penalty will then be measured from the succeeding spot. The penalty for any nonplayer or unsportsmanlike foul is administered from the succeeding spot. When there is a double foul during the down, the penalties offset and, in effect, there is no acceptance or declination of them.

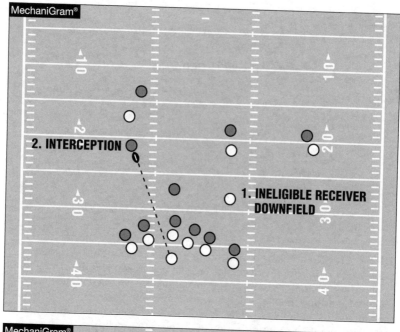

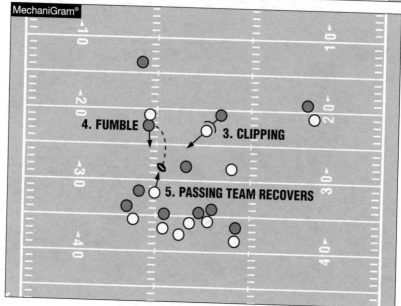

10-2-1b This is a double foul. The team gaining final possession had fouled prior to gaining final possession. The penalties cancel and the down will be replayed from the previous spot. When a double foul occurs, the captains are not consulted since the penalties offset automatically even in those cases where the penalty distances are not the same.

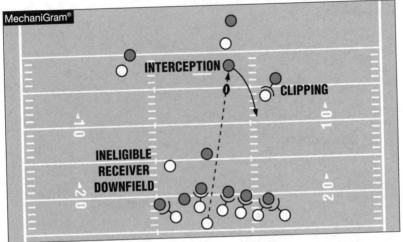

10-2-2 Live-ball fouls by opponents do not always combine to make a double foul. When there is a change of team possession and the team gaining final possession has not fouled prior to gaining possession and declines the penalty for its opponent's foul, that team may retain possession. If B declines the foul for A's ineligible receiver downfield, B will put the ball in play first and 10 following the administration of the penalty for clipping.

10-4 If Team K takes the field goal, the penalty for roughing will be enforced from the succeeding spot. Team K may instead accept the penalty resulting in an automatic first down, plus the distance penalty, which could put them in position to go for a touchdown. If the foul is flagrant, the offender is disqualified whether or not the penalty is accepted.

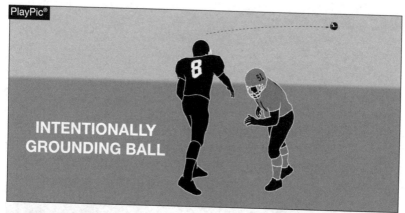

INTENTIONALLY GROUNDING BALL

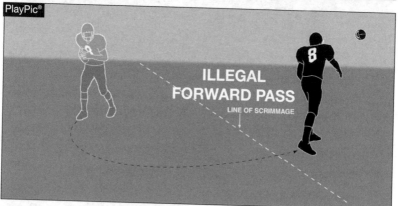

ILLEGAL FORWARD PASS

LINE OF SCRIMMAGE

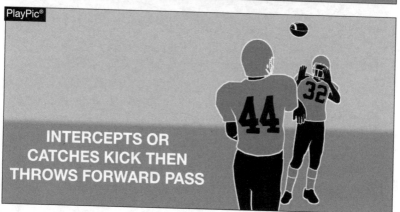

INTERCEPTS OR CATCHES KICK THEN THROWS FORWARD PASS

10-4-4 Since all illegal forward passes are running plays, the penalty, if accepted in any of these plays, will be enforced from the end of the related run. The down will count unless the forward pass was thrown after a change of possession during the down. Following a change of possession, a loss-of-down penalty has no significance.

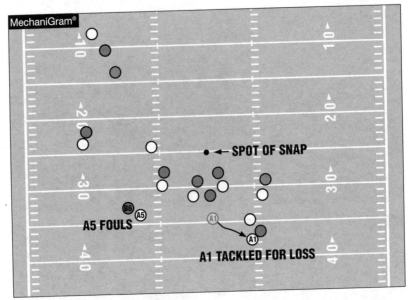

10-4-4 When a foul for offensive holding occurs during a running play and the foul is in advance of the basic spot it is penalized from the basic spot, which is the end of the related run.

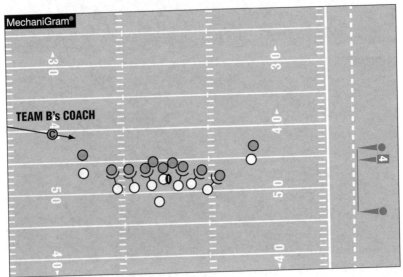

10-4-5a Team A is short of a first down on a fourth-down run. The penalty for the dead-ball unsportsmanlike foul on the Team B coach is administered before the line to gain is established for Team B. It will be first and 10 for B from its own 33-yard line.

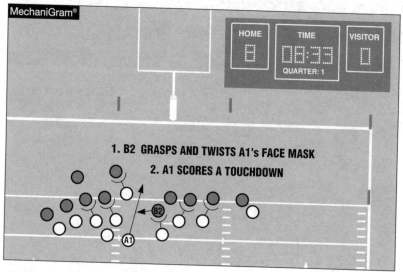

1. B2 GRASPS AND TWISTS A1's FACE MASK

2. A1 SCORES A TOUCHDOWN

10-5-1f, 8-2-2 If a live-ball defensive foul occurs during a touchdown-scoring play when there is no change of possession, the scoring team may accept the results of the play and have the penalty enforced from the succeeding spot or on the subsequent kickoff.

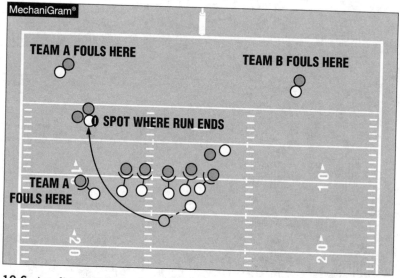

TEAM A FOULS HERE

TEAM B FOULS HERE

SPOT WHERE RUN ENDS

TEAM A FOULS HERE

10-6 Any live-ball foul, other than a nonplayer or unsportsmanlike foul or a foul simultaneous with the snap, is penalized according to the all-but-one enforcement principle. All fouls are penalized from the basic spot, except the foul by the offense which occurs behind the spot. In that case the penalty is administered from the spot of the foul.

OFFICIAL FOOTBALL SIGNALS

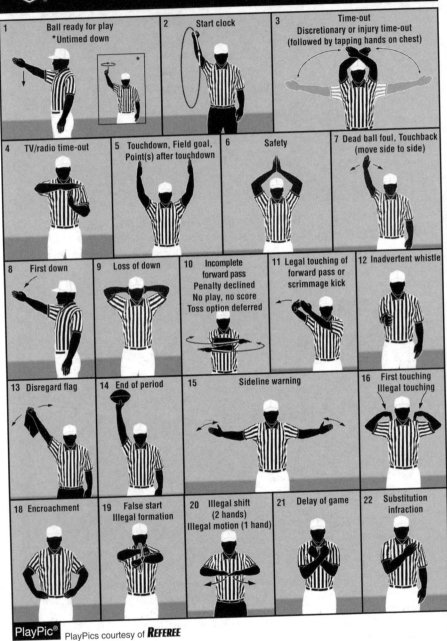

#	Signal
1	Ball ready for play *Untimed down
2	Start clock
3	Time-out Discretionary or injury time-out (followed by tapping hands on chest)
4	TV/radio time-out
5	Touchdown, Field goal, Point(s) after touchdown
6	Safety
7	Dead ball foul, Touchback (move side to side)
8	First down
9	Loss of down
10	Incomplete forward pass Penalty declined No play, no score Toss option deferred
11	Legal touching of forward pass or scrimmage kick
12	Inadvertent whistle
13	Disregard flag
14	End of period
15	Sideline warning
16	First touching Illegal touching
18	Encroachment
19	False start Illegal formation
20	Illegal shift (2 hands) Illegal motion (1 hand)
21	Delay of game
22	Substitution infraction

PlayPic® PlayPics courtesy of REFEREE

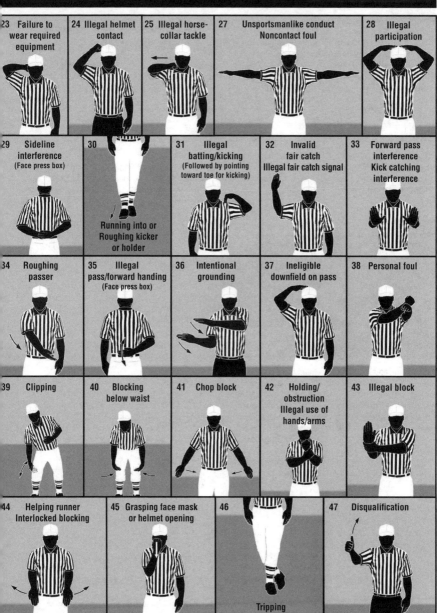

23 Failure to wear required equipment

24 Illegal helmet contact

25 Illegal horse-collar tackle

27 Unsportsmanlike conduct Noncontact foul

28 Illegal participation

29 Sideline interference (Face press box)

30 Running into or Roughing kicker or holder

31 Illegal batting/kicking (Followed by pointing toward toe for kicking)

32 Invalid fair catch Illegal fair catch signal

33 Forward pass interference Kick catching interference

34 Roughing passer

35 Illegal pass/forward handing (Face press box)

36 Intentional grounding

37 Ineligible downfield on pass

38 Personal foul

39 Clipping

40 Blocking below waist

41 Chop block

42 Holding/ obstruction Illegal use of hands/arms

43 Illegal block

44 Helping runner Interlocked blocking

45 Grasping face mask or helmet opening

46 Tripping

47 Disqualification

PlayPic®   PlayPics courtesy of REFEREE   Note: Signal numbers 17 and 26 is for future expansion.

PlayPic®

Double stakes	11 players	Snapper protection	Unbalanced line
			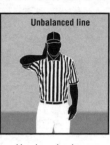

Indicates that more than ten yards to go before first down, to prevent accidental stopping of clock.

Fist at shoulder level, indication of 11 players in game when counting complete.

Indicates to each other (R and U) that this play requires protection for snapper in accordance with rules.

Hand on cheek, indicating unbalanced line to trigger all to look for ineligibles and umpire to check numbering. Also used for indicating two or more players or no players outside the tackle on the line of scrimmage.

PlayPic®

Last play was out of bounds	Backward pass

Arms extended below waist with palms toward sideline, outside of body. Last play was out of bounds (start clock on snap).

Given by R unless immediately thrown after snap in which case wing has crew option to signal. NO signal if forward. Also, same signal by wing officials to indicate player nearest wing official is off the line of scrimmage.

2013 NFHS Football Rules
Penalty Summary

LOSS OF 5 YARDS

SIGNAL

Failure to properly wear mandatory player equipment during down 27-23

Delay of game 7-21

Failure to properly wear mandatory player equipment just before snap . . . 7-21-23

Illegal substitution 22

Free-kick infraction 7-19

Encroachment 7-18

Free kick out of bounds 19

Invalid or illegal fair-catch signal 32

Snap infraction 7-19

False start 7-19

Illegal formation 19

Less than seven players on A's line or numbering violation 19

Illegal shift or illegal motion 20

Planned loose-ball infraction 19

Illegally handing ball forward (also loss of down) 35-9

Illegal forward pass (by A) (also loss of down) 35-9

Illegal forward pass (by B) 35

Intentional grounding (also loss of down) 36-9

Ineligible receiver illegally downfield 37

Illegal touching (also loss of down) 16-9

Helping runner 44

Incidental grasping of opponent's face mask (or any helmet opening, chin strap
or attached tooth and mouth protector) 45

Running into kicker/holder 30

Sideline interference 7-29

Attendant illegally on field 19

Nonplayer outside of the team box, but not on field 7-29

LOSS OF 10 YARDS

Illegal blocking technique 42

Interlocked blocking 44

LOSS OF 15 YARDS

DISQUALIFICATION ASSOCIATED WITH CERTAIN 15-YARD PENALTIES

COACHES-OFFICIALS

MEMBERSHIP INFORMATION

NFHS Coaches Association
NFHS Officials Association

ONE COACH AND ONE OFFICIAL SERVE ON EACH NFHS RULES COMMITTEE!

GENERAL LIABILITY INSURANCE

AVAILABILITY OF ONLINE PUBLICATIONS

AWARDS AND RECOGNITION!

──────────────── JOIN NOW ────────────────

Mr/Mrs/Ms: _____ First Name: _____ M.I. _____ Last Name: _____
                        (as it appears on your driver's license)

Home Address: _____ This is a new address ☐

City: _____ State/Province: _____ Zip: _____

Country: _____ Fax: ( ) _____

School/Organization Phone: ( ) _____ Home Phone: ( ) _____

For Insurance Purposes:
Birthdate: _____ ☐ Male ☐ Female

E-Mail Address: _____

Primary area of interest/expertise (sport) _____
First Year Officiating _____
First Year Coaching _____

CHECK TYPE OF MEMBERSHIP
☐ **COACH** $35.00
☐ **OFFICIAL** $40.00
   (Residents of foreign countries add $9.00 mailing costs)

☐ Check ☐ VISA ☐ MasterCard ☐ American Express

Account No.: _____ - _____ - _____ - _____

Exp. Date: _____ Card Security Code: _____
(call your merchant card provider for location of code.)

I WORK PRIMARILY IN: *(Check only one)*

☐ High School Sports
☐ College Sports
☐ Youth League Sports

DO NOT MAIL FORM WITHOUT PAYMENT
One annual payment provides member
benefits for one year from the date payment
is received by the NFHS.

Mail Payment to: NFHS
        PO Box 690
        Indianapolis, IN 46206

Cardholder Name _____ Signature _____

No purchase orders accepted   TOTAL AMOUNT ENCLOSED $_____

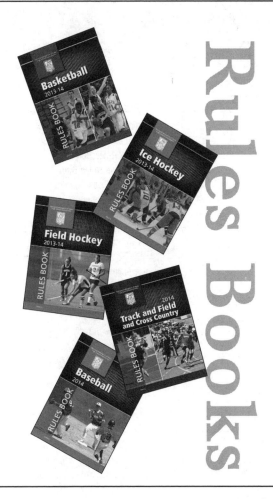

Baseball • Basketball • Field Hockey • Football • Girls Gymnastics

Ice Hockey • Boys Lacrosse • Soccer • Softball • Spirit

Swimming and Diving/Water Polo • Track and Field/Cross Country

• Volleyball • Wrestling

NFHS PUBLICATIONS

Prices effective April 1, 2013 — March 31, 2014

RULES PUBLICATIONS

Baseball Rules Book $7.20	Girls Gymnastics Rules Book & Manual (2012-14)
Baseball Case Book $7.20	.... $7.20
Baseball Umpires Manual (2013 & 2014).. $7.20	Ice Hockey Rules Book $7.20
Baseball Simplified & Illustrated Rules $8.95	Boys Lacrosse Rules Book $7.20
Baseball Rules by Topic $8.95	Soccer Rules Book $7.20
Basketball Rules Book $7.20	Softball Rules Book $7.20
Basketball Case Book $7.20	Softball Case Book $7.20
Basketball Simplified & Illustrated Rules ... $8.95	Softball Umpires Manual (2014 & 2015) ... $7.20
Basketball Officials Manual (2013-15) $7.20	Spirit Rules Book $7.20
Basketball Handbook (2012-14) $7.20	Swimming/Diving/Water Polo Rules Book . $7.20
Basketball Rules by Topic $7.95	Track & Field Rules Book $7.20
Field Hockey Rules Book $7.20	Track & Field Case Book $7.20
Football Rules Book $7.20	Track & Field Manual (2013 & 2014) $7.20
Football Case Book $7.20	Volleyball Rules Book $7.20
Football Simplified & Illustrated Rules $8.95	Volleyball Case Book & Manual $7.20
Football Handbook (2013 & 2014) $7.20	Wrestling Rules Book $7.20
Football Officials Manual (2012 & 2013) ... $7.20	Wrestling Case Book & Manual $7.20
Football Rules by Topic $8.95	

MISCELLANEOUS ITEMS

NFHS Statisticians' Manual $6.75

Scorebooks: Baseball-Softball, Basketball, Swimming & Diving, Cross Country, Soccer, Track & Field, Gymnastics, Volleyball, Wrestling and Field Hockey..$11.20

Diving Scoresheets (pad of 100)...$7.25

Volleyball Team Rosters & Lineup Sheets (pads of 100) $7.25

Libero Tracking Sheet (pads of 50) $7.25

Baseball/Softball Lineup Sheets - 3-Part NCR (sets/100) $8.75

Wrestling Tournament Match Cards (sets/100)...$7.25

Flipping Coin $5.50

NFHS Pin..$4.00

Competitors Numbers (Track and Gymnastics – Waterproof, nontearable, black numbers and six colors of backgrounds

    Numbers are 1-1000 sold in sets of 100 ....$15.00/set

Lane Numbers (1-8), size 4" x 2 1/2" $7.25/set

MISCELLANEOUS SPORTS ITEMS

Court and Field Diagram Guide $20.20	Sportsmanship. It's Up to You. Toolkit......$19.95
NFHS Handbook (2013-14) $9.00	High School Activities — A Community
Let's Make It Official $5.00	Investment in America........................$39.95

2013-14 NFHS ORDER BLANK

Name _____ Phone _____

School and/or Organization _____

Address _____

_____
City   State   Zip

(No PO Boxes. If charging order to a credit card please use address on card.)
If address has changed in the last year please fill in old address.

_____
Street   City   State   Zip

Check one of the following: ☐ Visa ☐ MasterCard

Account No. _____ - _____ - _____ - _____ Exp. Date_____

Signature _____

P.O. # _____ (Order totals $50 or more)
(attach P.O.)

Item#	Description	Quantity	Unit Price	Total

SHIPPING & HANDLING CHARGES: If your subtotal is:

$1.00 to $15.00 ....add **$7.95** $75.01 to $100.00 ...add **$15.95**
$15.01 to $25.00 ....add **$9.95** $100.01 to $250.00 .add **$18.95**
$25.01 to $50.00 .....add **$10.95** $250.01 to $500.00 .add **$21.95**
$50.01 to $75.00 .....add **$12.95**   Over $500.01 add 5% of subtotal
Second Day = Standard shipping charges plus **$15.00**
Overnight = Standard shipping charges plus **$25.00**
All shipments to Alaska, Hawaii, Virgin Islands and Canada – add **$10.00**
Call for charges outside continental U.S.

Subtotal _____

Shipping &
Handling Charge _____

TOTAL _____

Send to: NFHS CUSTOMER SERVICE
PO Box 361246, INDIANAPOLIS, IN 46236-5324
Phone 800-776-3462, Fax 317.899.7496 or online at www.nfhs.com

ORDERING INFORMATION

PURCHASE ORDERS are welcomed but all orders under $50 must be prepaid. Purchase orders may be **either faxed or mailed** to our Customer Service office. If you mail a purchase order after it has been faxed to our Customer Service office, please show it as a **confirming order**. All back-ordered items will be billed additional shipping charges. Terms net 30 days per invoice. All delinquent accounts are charged 1.5% finance charges. **PREPAID ORDERS** will be shipped upon receipt of completed order form accompanied by a check or money order. **All orders must include the proper amount for shipping and handling.**
*SHIPMENTS OUTSIDE UNITED STATES OR CANADA: Please write to NFHS headquarters for a quotation of total charges which will include a $2.00 surcharge and actual shipping charges. **Payment must be in U.S. dollars.** Please refer to www.nfhs.com to view our Return Policy.

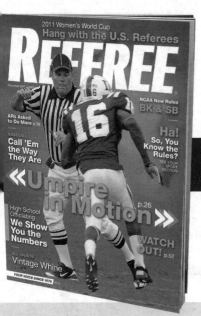